M.L.K.

JOURNEY OF A KING

By Tonya Bolden

Photo editor: Bob Adelman

Abrams Books for Young Readers

New York

IN MEMORY OF DAVID RUSSELL HACKLEY (1957–2005)

Founder and CEO of World Peace Communications, whose love for photography knew no bounds

Library of Congress Cataloging-in-Publication Data:

Bolden, Tonya.

M.L.K.: journey of a King / by Tonya Bolden; photography editor, Bob Adelman.

p. cm.

ISBN 13: 978-0-8109-5476-2

ISBN 10: 0-8109-5476-1

1. King, Martin Luther, Jr., 1929–1968—Juvenile literature. 2. African
Americans—Biography—Juvenile literature. 3. Civil rights workers—United
States—Biography—Juvenile literature. 4. Baptists—United
States—Biography—Juvenile literature. 5. African Americans—Civil
rights—History—20th century—Juvenile literature. I. Adelman, Bob, ill.

II. Title.

E185.97.K5B595 2006

323.092—dc22

[B]

2006013332

Book design by Celina Carvalho

Production manager: Alexis Mentor

Published in 2007 by Abrams Books for Young Readers, an imprint of Harry N. Abrams, Inc. All rights reserved.

Printed and bound in China

10 9 8 7 6 5 4

ABRAMS The Art of Books
115 West 18th Street, New York, NY 10011
abramsbooks.com

CONTENTS

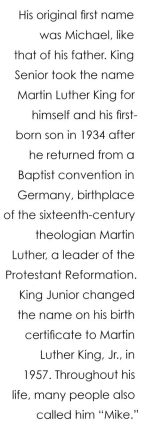

His original first name was Michael, like that of his father. King Senior took the name Martin Luther King for himself and his first-born son in 1934 after he returned from a Baptist convention in Germany, birthplace of the sixteenth-century theologian Martin Luther, a leader of the Protestant Reformation. King Junior changed the name on his birth certificate to Martin Luther King, Jr., in 1957. Throughout his life, many people also called him "Mike."

WEEK OF SHOCK
- Vietnam: Burst of Hope
- Convulsion in U.S. Politics
- EXCLUSIVE PICTURES
  The Murder in Memphis

These words, white type on black, headlined the April 12, 1968, issue of *Life* magazine. Inside, readers received details on possible peace talks between North and South Vietnam and insights on President Johnson's bombshell of an announcement that he would not seek reelection. Deeper into the magazine, a photo essay on the murder in Memphis appears.

Most riveting and remembered is the photograph of a scene on a balcony of the Lorraine Motel. People point toward a boardinghouse across the way. You can almost hear them shout, *Over there! Over there!* At their feet, a downed man. A white towel covers his rifle-shot shattered jaw.

"Oh." One eyewitness believed that was the last word the man tried to say. About an hour later, he was pronounced dead.

"M.L." his father had nicknamed him. "M.L." he had called himself, keeping it simple long before his life became so intense.

"Oh"?

If so, as in *Oh, no, I don't want to go!* or as in *Oh, my God!,* beholding the Shekinah Glory?

Oh.

As his blood haloed around his head, perhaps life notes flashed across his mental sky and he saw the boy he once was: so grieved by the sight of desperate souls in Great Depression breadlines; so free from poverty's claws, thanks to dutiful, domineering Daddy; so nourished into a sense of somebodiness by mild-mannered Mother Dear. Much love was also lavished on him by Mother Dear's mother. Her eyes shined brightest at the sight of him, he sensed, and her illness, then death, had him jumping from a second-story window of his home, leaving people to puzzle whether it was a foolish attempt to prove himself brave or a desire to die because he could not bear the pain.

> . . . so grieved by the sight of desperate souls in Great Depression breadlines; so free from poverty's claws thanks to dutiful, domineering Daddy; so nourished into a sense of somebodiness by mild-mannered Mother Dear. Much love was also lavished on him by Mother Dear's mother.

Oh.

As the fire shut up in M.L.'s bones embered, perhaps he heard his young self singing in the choir—church so ever present in his life, like water for fish, but his soul unconvinced. He only answered the altar call because his big sister had. In Sunday school, he once voiced doubt about a bottom-line belief for most Christians: that Jesus literally rose from the dead.

Oh.

**M.L.'S FIRST HOME:
501 AUBURN AVENUE, N.E.,
ATLANTA, GEORGIA**

M.L.'s older sister and younger brother were also born in this house, where their parents began their married life in 1926. The house belonged to their mother's parents: Jennie Celeste Parks Williams, a native of Atlanta, and Reverend Adam Daniel "A.D." Williams, born near Penfield, Georgia. When A.D. Williams moved to Atlanta in 1893, he was already a licensed Baptist preacher. A year later, he became pastor of the eight-year-old Ebenezer Baptist Church, which had about a dozen members. Ten years later, membership topped seven hundred. Reverend Williams attended Atlanta Baptist College (renamed Morehouse College in 1913). He cofounded the Georgia Equal Rights League and the Atlanta branch of the National Association for the Advancement of Colored People (NAACP).

**SEPARATE
AND UNEQUAL**

The United States Supreme Court sanctioned racial segregation in its 1896 ruling in *Plessy v. Ferguson*. The court maintained that as long as facilities were equal, there was no problem. Facilities for blacks, from schools to water fountains, were never equal to those for whites. Inequality reinforced the notion of inferiority, as did the nonexistence in some localities of public libraries, swimming pools, and other facilities for blacks. Segregation, also known as Jim Crow, was blatant and ubiquitous in the South—and long-lasting, as evidenced by this photo taken inside a Louisiana courthouse in 1964.

As M.L. lay dying, he may have glimpsed snippets of distant days when racism cut him to the quick, as happened when a white man who owned a store near his home banned his son's friendship with M.L. shortly before the boys started elementary school—the white boy going to one for whites, M.L. to one for blacks. There was the day a clerk wouldn't let him try on a pair of shoes unless he and his father took seats in the back of the store. On another day, at age eight, he stood outside a different store waiting for Mother Dear with his face and spirit stinging from a white woman's slap and slander: "You are that nigger that stepped on my foot."

[There was the day a clerk wouldn't let him try on a pair of shoes unless he and his father took seats in the back of the store.]

Oh.

His parents kept constant vigil over their children's psyches, cheering them as children of promise and counseling them not to hate whites, but instead to love them with the love that Jesus preached. *How could I love a race of people who hated me?* young M.L. wondered, intent on hating white folks forever.

During a youth filled with all-American traditions and pursuits—family dinners, Christmas gifts, baseball games, a paper route—other incidents fueled his resolve to hate, such as seeing members of the Ku Klux Klan (KKK) beat a black man and white cops abuse black youth; being unable to play in public parks; and being forced to ride in the back of the city bus to and from high school. One mid-April 1944 day he and a teacher, Mrs. Bradley, stood for most of the ninety-mile journey from Dublin, Georgia, to Atlanta because the bus driver had ordered them to surrender their seats to whites, then cursed at them for not moving quickly. M.L. had wanted to sit tight, but his teacher convinced him that nothing good would come of defying the segregation law behind the bus driver's demand. M.L. seethed all the way home, stripped of his joy. For in Dublin, he had done well in an oratorical contest with his speech "The Negro and the Constitution," a plea for racial justice.

PRECIOUS MEMORIES

The far right photo was taken in January 1939. Seated, left to right: M.L.'s brother, Alfred Daniel, called "A.D." (born 1930); sister Willie Christine, called "Christine" (born 1927); and M.L. (born 1929). Behind the children, left, their "Mother Dear," Alberta Christine Williams King, a graduate of Morris Brown College, and their father, "Daddy King," who was very active with the NAACP. At age eighteen this son of sharecroppers in Stockbridge, Georgia, moved to Atlanta with nothing but ambition. He not only won the heart of A.D. Williams's daughter, but also became assistant pastor of his church. Along the way, King Senior attended Morehouse College. After his father-in-law died in March 1931, he became pastor of Ebenezer. Next to Daddy King, M.L.'s beloved maternal grandmother, who died when he was twelve. Shortly after her death, the King family moved into a house a few blocks away from the one on Auburn Avenue.

YOUNG M.L. IN THE NEWS

From the April 16, 1944, issue of the *Atlanta Daily World*, one of the most successful black-owned newspapers in the South. M.L. was a junior at Booker T. Washington High when he won the speech contest mentioned here. With another student, he earned the honor of representing his school in the statewide contest held in a church in Dublin, Georgia, on April 17.

Contest Winner

M. L. KING, Jr.
The elimination contest of the Washington high school, under the direction of the committee on Elks' orations, was held at the Service Men's Center Thursday morning at 10 30 o'clock.

In September 1944, M.L. was a Morehouse Man. He had already skipped ninth grade, and after passing Morehouse College's early-entrance exam, he was allowed to skip twelfth grade. Because World War II—and the draft—was still on, Morehouse, like other colleges, was hungry for students. And though M.L. was bright, the fifteen-year-old college freshman was hardly a stellar student: He was reading on an eighth grade level; his grasp of grammar wasn't firm. Early on in college, he was content with mediocre grades, spending a lot of his energy on snappy dressing and chatting up girls around town.

M.L. wasn't all flash and flirt, however, and at Morehouse just about every professor was on fire to inspire students to lives of service to the black community. When M.L. looked into his future, he initially saw himself doing this as a doctor, then as a lawyer. He resisted people's expectation, especially his father's, that he become a minister. He bristled against his family's brand of Christianity because it frowned upon things he enjoyed, like dancing. He also had doubts that everything in the Bible really happened. As for the expressive Baptist worship style: "[T]he shouting and the stamping. I didn't understand it and it embarrassed me," he admitted years later.

MOREHOUSE MEN

M.L.'s extracurricular activities included membership in the college's glee club, basketball team, and NAACP chapter. He also joined an interracial organization of area college students concerned with issues of the day. Participation in that group persuaded him that not all whites, especially in his generation, were hostile to racial justice. M.L. (second row, third from left) majored in sociology, the study of societies. Brother A.D. also attended Morehouse. Christine went to Spelman College, Morehouse's sister school.

BENJAMIN ELIJAH MAYS

A South Carolina native whose parents were born into slavery, Mays earned his B.A. from Bates College in Maine, and his M.A. and Ph.D. from the University of Chicago. When he became president of Morehouse in 1940, he worked tirelessly to transform the school from a respectable institution of higher learning into *the* leading historically black college for men. Mays was a vigorous champion of the concept of a Morehouse Man as someone who strives for excellence and lives not for himself alone.

A course on the Bible with Morehouse alumnus George Kelsey, head of its religion department, sparked a great awakening. Like M.L.'s father, Kelsey was an adherent to the social gospel: the belief that Christians shouldn't be so heavenly minded to the point of not being engaged in fighting for a just society. But unlike M.L.'s father, Professor Kelsey did not flinch from critical analysis of the Scriptures. M.L. continued to question some things in the Bible, but after studying with Kelsey, he was satisfied that it contained "many profound truths which one could not escape." Kelsey spurred him to reconsider his rejection of the ministry, as did another man M.L. revered: Morehouse's president, Benjamin Mays. "Both were ministers, both deeply religious, and yet both were learned men, aware of all the trends in modern thinking. I could see in their lives the ideal of what I wanted a minister to be." By the time M.L. graduated from college in 1948, he had been ordained and become associate pastor of Ebenezer, his family's church.

In M.L.'s quest to be a minister like Kelsey and Mays, he opted for Crozer Theological Seminary, a small, predominantly white Baptist school in Chester, Pennsylvania. In his third and final year, he pulled down a string of A's and was student-body president, shining at graduation as valedictorian and recipient of an award for most outstanding student in his class. Another award came with a $1,200 grant for graduate school. For him that was Boston University's School of Theology, where he would earn a Ph.D. in systematic theology, the study of Christianity's core beliefs and teachings. Along the way, he met the smart, talented, and stunning Coretta Scott, who became his wife.

> "Both were ministers, both deeply religious, and yet both were learned men, aware of all the trends in modern thinking. I could see in their lives the ideal of what I wanted a minister to be."

Coretta was born in Heiberger, Alabama (near Marion), into a family of modest means and giant pride. While she was a student at Antioch College in Yellow Springs, Ohio, she participated in some Progressive Party events. The party's agenda included increased federal spending on education, universal health care, a minimum wage for all workers, and an end to segregation. After Coretta graduated from Antioch in 1951, she went to the New England Conservatory of Music in Boston, pursuing her dream of being a concert singer. There, she met M.L.

When M.L. and Coretta married in June 1953, he was done with his course work and exams. He still had to complete his dissertation (a long research paper), but he didn't have to remain in Boston to do that. So he thought about his horizons. Professor? Pastor? He also seesawed between returning to the South and remaining in the North, where racism and segregation were generally less blatant. His father wanted him to become co-pastor of Ebenezer. His wife wanted to remain in the North. M.L. disappointed them both when he accepted the pastorate of Dexter Avenue Baptist Church in Montgomery, Alabama.

> "I have no pretense to being a great preacher or even a profound scholar. I certainly have no pretense to infallibility . . ."

"I come to you with nothing so special to offer," M.L. said in his first sermon as Dexter's pastor on Sunday, May 2, 1954. "I have no pretense to being a great preacher or even a profound scholar. I certainly have no pretense to infallibility . . . I come to you with only the claim of being a servant of Christ, and a feeling of dependence on his grace for my leadership." He spoke of having felt like the Old Testament prophet Jeremiah, who had likened the word of God in his heart to "burning fire shut up in my bones."

About two weeks after that sermon, hope of imminent deliverance from segregation and its attendant humiliations was aflame in the hearts of millions of blacks. The U.S. Supreme Court declared segregated public school systems unconstitutional in its ruling in *Brown v. Board of Education*, a case made possible by the legal arm of the NAACP. The ruling renewed the strength of people who had labored for the abolition of segregation for years; it inspired others to get active in a civil rights crusade as old as the nation.

**DEXTER AVENUE
BAPTIST CHURCH:
454 DEXTER AVENUE,
MONTGOMERY,
ALABAMA**

M.L. would later say
that he returned to
the South because he
felt that was where
he could be of most
service to his people.
The fact that Dexter,
though small, was a
prestigious church
in the black Baptist
world, probably had
something to do with
his decision.

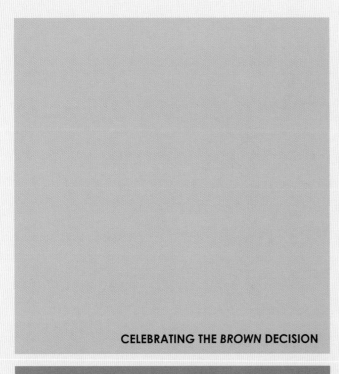

CELEBRATING THE BROWN DECISION

The NAACP's chief attorney, Thurgood Marshall (center), with fellow lawyers George E.C. Hayes (left) and James Nabrit, Jr., outside the U.S. Supreme Court on May 17, 1954, shortly after the historic ruling.

M.L. was a member of the NAACP and urged all members of his congregation who weren't members to join, but he had no plans for intense activism. He focused on finishing his dissertation (delivered in April 1955) and fulfilling his duties to Dexter. Being a good father was added to the list in mid-November 1955, when Coretta gave birth to their first child, Yolanda. M.L. nicknamed her "Yoki."

M.L.'s plan to lead a rather predictable life fell by the wayside when local activists rushed to wring something transformative out of Rosa Parks's arrest on Thursday, December 1, 1955, for refusing to yield her bus seat to a white person. They called for a boycott of the city buses on the day of Parks's trial, Monday, December 5.

When NAACP stalwart Edgar Daniel "E.D." Nixon telephoned M.L. on Friday morning asking him to support the boycott, M.L. hesitated—"Let me think about it awhile"—but he didn't stay on the sidelines for long. On Saturday night, December 3, he joined a spread-the-word brigade that drove around to entertainment joints to get folks to back Monday's boycott and show up at a mass meeting that evening at Holt Street Baptist Church. On Sunday morning, M.L. urged the same at Dexter. When he went to bed that night, he did so "with a strange mixture of hope and anxiety," he later wrote. When hardly any blacks rode the buses on Monday morning, "a miracle had taken place."

JO ANN GIBSON ROBINSON

On the night of Parks's arrest, Robinson and some friends were up half the night secretly running off thousands of copies of a leaflet about the boycott on the mimeograph machine at Alabama State College, where she taught English. The leaflet ended with the plea "But please, children and grown-ups, don't ride the bus at all on Monday. Please stay off of all buses Monday." Robinson, a member of Dexter and president of the Women's Political Council, had called for a bus boycott many months earlier.

A MONTGOMERY CITY LINES BUS

Blacks comprised about 70 percent of bus ridership in Montgomery. In addition to having to sit in the back of the bus, blacks first had to board at the front of the bus to pay their fares, then get off and reboard at the back door. Bus drivers sometimes drove off before a black person could get back on the bus. Some drivers verbally and physically assaulted black passengers.

On Monday afternoon, M.L. was at the meeting that gave birth to an organization to shepherd the miracle: the Montgomery Improvement Association (MIA). He was shocked to find himself the unanimous choice for MIA president, but something within wouldn't let him say no. He left the meeting with about thirty minutes to come up with a speech for the mass meeting, where MIA would find out if folks were up for more than a one-day stand.

When M.L. reached home, he briefed his wife about his MIA presidency, then hurried to draft his speech. After several minutes in pure panic, "I turned to God in prayer. My words were brief and simple, asking God to restore my balance and to be with me in a time when I needed His guidance more than ever." He left home with just an outline in his head.

As Rosa Parks made her way through the throng outside Holt Street Baptist Church on that December 5 evening, she sensed that "something powerful was being born." Inside, the meeting commenced with song: "Onward Christian Soldiers" and "Leaning on the Everlasting Arms." There was a prayer by Willie Alford, pastor of Beulah Baptist Church. Uriah Fields, pastor of Bell Street Baptist Church, offered the Scripture reading: Psalm 34, a praise song for deliverance from trials and tribulations.

FOUND GUILTY

At her trial on December 5, Rosa Parks was found guilty of disorderly conduct and fined fourteen dollars. With her, left to right: E.D. Nixon and attorney Fred Gray. He is informing an official of his intent to appeal Parks's conviction.

When M.L. addressed the crowd at Holt Street Baptist Church, he recapped what had happened to Rosa Parks and alluded to indignities other blacks routinely endured. His voice was calm, even-toned, businesslike. But he soon shifted into Baptist preacher mode—singsonging phrases, rolling out repetitions, giving in to the body-rock.

"And you know, my friends, there comes a time when people get tired of being trampled over by the iron feet of oppression."

Thunderous applause forced him to pause.

"There comes a time, my friends, when people get tired of being plunged across the abyss of humiliation, where they experience the bleakness of nagging despair."

"Keep talkin'!" a man shouted out.

"There comes a time when people get tired of being pushed out of the glittering sunlight of life's July and left standing amid the piercing chill of an alpine November."

> "And you know, my friends, there comes a time when people get tired of being trampled over by the iron feet of oppression."

The crowd was a hallelujah chorus. People clapped their hands, stamped their feet. They hollered out for M.L. to preach on. This display of emotion hardly embarrassed him as it might have done in his youth. He became a roar: "And we are not wrong, we are not wrong in what we are doing. If we are wrong, the Supreme Court of this nation is wrong. If we are wrong, the Constitution of the United States is wrong. If we are wrong, God Almighty is wrong." He called on the crowd "to work and fight until justice runs down like water and righteousness like a mighty stream." He underscored unity: "[I]f we are united we can get many of the things that we not only desire but which we justly deserve." He urged grace: "Let us be Christian in all of our actions." If the people abided by these principles, M.L. ventured that "when the history books are written in the future, somebody will have to say, 'There lived a race of people, a *black* people . . . a people who had

**DECEMBER 5, 1955:
HOLT STREET
BAPTIST CHURCH**

The church was packed. Outside, thousands listened to the proceedings via loudspeakers.

the moral courage to stand up for their rights. And thereby they injected a new meaning into the veins of history and civilization.'"

Something powerful was born that night alright. The crowd committed to supporting MIA's demands and to continuing the boycott until they were met. The number-one demand was not for an end to segregated seating, but rather an end to blacks being forced to give up their seats to whites if there were no empty seats in the whites-only front of the bus. MIA also called for blacks to be treated with respect and for the bus company to hire black drivers for predominantly black routes.

SHARE-A-RIDE

Carpooling succeeded early on because people who never rode the buses (people like M.L.) lent their cars to the cause. For tips on organizing and maintaining a car-pool system, MIA reached out to Reverend T.J. Jemison, a leader of the June 1953 bus boycott in Baton Rouge, Louisiana. MIA eventually purchased a number of station wagons. Donations, large and small, from individuals and civic, social, and religious organizations around the country helped pay for these cars, their repairs, gasoline, and other expenses. A cash-poor, unemployed woman in Boise, Idaho, sent two pairs of her shoes because some boycotters walked, from one to more than ten miles a day. To keep spirits up, MIA held mass meetings at least once a week, rotating them from church to church.

What began as a one-day boycott became days upon days of sacrifice: day laborers and domestic workers walking, seamstresses and janitors piling into pickup trucks and sedans, students and schoolteachers huddling up with

THE "GET-TOUGH" POLICY

A few weeks into the boycott, cops began ticketing and arresting blacks for trivial and trumped-up violations. Some people who were waiting for rides were charged with loitering, for example. On January 26, 1956, while he was giving people rides, M.L. was pulled over and taken to jail for allegedly doing thirty miles per hour in a twenty-five-mile-per-hour zone. He wasn't in jail for long. As the crowd of blacks around the jail thickened, the head jailer released him.

friends and near-strangers at car-pool spots. Black Montgomery, blue collar and bourgeoisie, showed amazing solidarity and steadfastness in the cold, whether drizzle or driving rain, despite news of acid thrown on a car, a brick through a window, dynamite across a family's front lawn, black-owned gas stations being bombed—and the city's refusal to budge.

Like others, M.L. discovered quickly what it felt like to be persecuted for the sake of righteousness. Jesus told his disciples that people who were wronged for doing right were blessed. It was tough to feel blessed on days when he received a slew of slurs and threats by telephone and mail. "If one day you find me sprawled out dead, I do not want you to retaliate with a single act of violence," he insisted at a mid-January 1956 rally. "I urge you to continue protesting with the same dignity and discipline you have shown so far."

Several days later, around midnight, when he answered his telephone: "Nigger, we are tired of you and your mess now. And if you aren't out of this town in three days, we're going to blow your brains out and blow up your house." Blessed? This threat unnerved him as none had before. Unable to sleep, he ended up in his kitchen, pacing some, worrying much. He fretted for a way "to move out of the picture without appearing a coward." He was doubled over with doubt about everything, including his faith. Yet, the only thing he had to lean on was prayer: "I am here taking a stand for what I believe is right. But now I am afraid . . . I am at the end of my powers." In a twinkling, he felt "the presence of the Divine" like never before. "It seemed as though I could hear the quiet assurance of an inner voice saying, 'Stand up for righteousness, stand up for truth, and God will be at your side forever.'"

And if you aren't out of this town in three days . . .

Three days later, on January 30, M.L. endorsed the more radical course several colleagues had advocated from the start: a lawsuit aimed at abolishing segregated seating.

And if you aren't out of this town in three days . . .

> "I am here taking a stand for what I believe is right. But now I am afraid . . . I am at the end of my powers."

HAPPY FAMILY

During his moment of crisis, M.L. was in knots about the harm that could befall not only him but also his wife and baby girl. He feared an end to happy family moments like this one, snapped a few months later outside Dexter, a short walk away from the capitol building.

That night, M.L. was at a mass meeting when told that his home had been bombed. Coretta and Yoki weren't physically hurt, but he didn't know that until he reached his house, where several hundred blacks had gathered in response to the bombing, more than a few of them armed with guns, knives, and broken bottles.

"Now let's not become panicky," M.L. told the people gathered around his home. "If you have weapons, take them home; if you do not have them, please do not seek to get them. We cannot solve this problem through retaliatory violence. We must meet violence with nonviolence . . . Jesus still cries out in words that echo across the centuries: '[L]ove your enemies; bless them that curse you; pray for them that despitefully use you.' This is what we must live by. We must meet hate with love." With him, left to right: Montgomery mayor W.A. Gayle, fire chief R.L. Lampley, and police commissioner Clyde Sellers. The mayor and the police chief had recently joined the city's White Citizens Council, an organization devoted to maintaining segregation.

M.L. did a masterful job of calming the crowd, but later that night, he was "on the verge of corroding hate." He dug deep for the strength to love. By then, he understood well what the love Jesus preached really meant. He knew that it was neither the kind of love that he felt for Yoki, his parents, or his friends, nor the kind of love he had for Coretta, but rather *agape*, (pronounced *ah-gah-pay*), a Greek word for a higher, harder love: a love that has nothing to do with liking a person, a love worthy of people who do you no good and even do you wrong. *Agape* says to see past a person's sins to the soul God loves.

SECURITY

Making M.L. and Coretta's home on South Jackson Street habitable again included repairing the hole in the porch, replacing the front window, installing floodlights, and arranging for security guards.

As M.L.'s commitment to *agape* intensified, so did the persecution. In February 1956, he and scores of other MIA leaders were charged with violating an Alabama anti-boycott law.

He was in Nashville for speaking engagements when the indictments were handed down. He promptly made plans to return to Montgomery. First, he had to jet to Atlanta to pick up Coretta and Yoki, who were staying with his parents. Stopping off in Atlanta meant dealing with his father's face-to-face pleas that he quit the Montgomery movement. His father feared for his son's life and for his own wife's well-being. Mother Dear had hardly left her bed since M.L.'s home was bombed.

["I must go back to Montgomery . . . I have begun the struggle, and I can't turn back. I have reached the point of no return."]

His father asked several pillars of the black community to come by the house to help him talk some sense into his son's head. Benjamin Mays was among them.

M.L. listened respectfully to his father and to those who seconded his father's sentiments, then told them, "I must go back to Montgomery. My friends and associates are being arrested. It would be the height of cowardice for me to stay away . . . I have begun the struggle, and I can't turn back. I have reached the point of no return." His father began sobbing. M.L. didn't know what to expect when he turned to Benjamin Mays.

"You're right, son," his mentor said.

M.L. had received—and would continue to receive—a raft of letters and telegrams of support from friends and strangers. "For years, we Negro Mothers of the Southland have prayed that God would send us a leader such as you are," Pinkie Franklin wrote shortly after M.L.'s home was bombed. This woman, a member of Sixteenth Street Baptist Church in Birmingham, also told him, "Day and night without ceasing I shall be praying for your safety and that of your [family]."

**BAND OF BROTHERS
AND SISTERS**

M.L. and other indicted MIA members stand before the Alabama State Capitol building (M.L. and other leaders are in the foreground). They regarded their indictment for violating an anti-boycott law as a badge of honor. The authorities thought the indictments would destabilize the movement, demoralize the people, and thereby break the boycott, but the plan backfired. It strengthened black Montgomery's resolve and netted the boycott more publicity. M.L. didn't care for the term "boycott." He preferred "noncooperation with evil."

**FEBRUARY 23, 1956:
MONTGOMERY
COUNTY JAIL**

Shortly after M.L. returned from Atlanta, he surrendered to the authorities. After he was booked, he was released on bond. His trial began on March 19.

"The people are with you," wrote Walter McCall, one of M.L.'s friends since Morehouse. McCall's letter was dated February 1, 1956, the same day that MIA attorney Fred Gray filed the lawsuit against segregated bus seating in U.S. District Court. That night, E.D. Nixon's home was bombed. Still, black Montgomery hung tough. Still, M.L. stayed the guiding light. Words of encouragement kept apace.

Frank Stanley, editor of the *Louisville Defender* and president of the oldest black fraternity, Alpha Phi Alpha, assured M.L. that some twenty thousand Alphas and millions of other blacks were behind him. "You have but to call on us, your Brothers, if we can be of any material assistance. We are already with you spiritually."

Crozer Theological Seminary's president, Sankey Blanton, wrote that the school saluted his "outstanding leadership."

"You and other leaders of this movement have been very right in insisting upon the peaceful, non-violent and loving nature of the struggle," wrote fellow Morehouse Man Charles Lawrence, chair of Fellowship of Reconciliation, a faith-based, interracial organization promoting human rights and world peace.

George Kelsey reminded M.L. that he had always been proud of him. "You surely can imagine my present feelings."

"NEGRO AND WHITE WAREHOUSEMEN IN SAN FRANCISCO BACK YOU IN COURAGEOUS FIGHT FOR DEMOCRACY IN SOUTH. KEEP SPIRITS UP AND STAY UNITED," read a telegram from a labor union officer.

M.L. heard from notables whom he did not know. One was Ralph Bunche, the first black recipient of the Nobel Peace Prize (1950), for his work as chair of the United Nations commission that brokered a truce between Israel and four Arab nations. In Bunche's telegram, he told M.L. that his determination, wisdom, and "QUIET COURAGE" constituted "AN INSPIRING CHAPTER IN THE HISTORY OF HUMAN DIGNITY."

In her letter, writer Lillian Smith asked M.L. to tell blacks in Montgomery that she was "deeply humbled" by their "goodwill, the self discipline, the courage, the wisdom." Smith, a white Southerner, also asked him to let his people know that she was doing her utmost to enlighten *her* people, trying to "open their hearts to the great harm that segregation inflicts not only on Negroes but on white people too."

MARCH 22, 1956:
THE TRIAL IS OVER

Found guilty, M.L. was ordered to pay a fine of $500, plus $500 in court costs, or spend 386 days in prison. His attorney immediately filed an appeal, and after a $1,000 bond was posted, M.L. was released. He, his wife, and their supporters are jubilant because they are proud of his "crime." "The protest is still on," M.L. declared at the mass meeting that night. "Whenever there is any great movement toward freedom, there will inevitably be some tension," he reminded the crowd. "You don't get to the Promised Land without going through the wilderness . . . Let us continue with the same spirit, with the same orderliness, with the same discipline, with the same Christian approach."

Some people started calling M.L. the black Gandhi, likening him to the father of India's independence from Great Britain. M.L., however, continued to consider himself uppermost a disciple of Christ, the proponent of nonviolence and "Prince of Peace" he began learning about as a child. Gandhi's greatness, however, was not lost on M.L.

GANDHI

In his day, Mohandas Karamchand Gandhi was the epic advocate of liberation through nonviolent direct action, also known as nonviolent resistance. It includes strikes, pickets, marches, and boycotts. The Mahatma ("Great Soul"), as his disciples hailed him, was assassinated on January 30, 1948, when M.L. was a senior at Morehouse.

Benjamin Mays had visited India in the 1930s and had often talked about Gandhi when M.L. was at Morehouse. While at Crozer, M.L. went to Philadelphia to hear the president of Howard University, Mordecai Johnson, deliver an address on the Mahatma. M.L. left that lecture more fascinated by Gandhi's use of boycotts, marches, and other acts of nonviolent protest powered by *satyagraha*, a Hindi word translated as *truth-force*, or *soul-force*, the term M.L. liked. But back then, M.L. didn't have much faith that what had worked in India could work in America. At the start of the boycott, he was not a true believer in total nonviolence. He had guns in his home for self-defense. Early on, he preached nonviolence to his followers in part for practical reasons: If blacks resorted to violence, the authorities might well call on the entire city police force, state troopers, and, if necessary, the National Guard.

During the boycott, at the urging of several pacifists around the nation, M.L. mused on Gandhi more and struggled to embrace nonviolence as a way of life, rejecting violence even in self-defense and repenting of having guns in his home. In interviews and speeches, he often capsuled the movement in Montgomery with this: "Christ furnished the spirit and motivation, while Gandhi furnished the method." And he thanked God, not Gandhi, for the victory.

While some forty thousand Montgomerians walked and carpooled and worked their soul-force, the boycott-inspired lawsuit made its way up to the U.S. Supreme Court. On November 13, 1956, it upheld a lower court's ruling that outlawed segregated seating on city buses in all of Alabama. On December 21, right after the law went into effect, the boycott would end after nearly four hundred days. In preparation, MIA sponsored an Institute on Nonviolence and Social Change at Holt Street Baptist Church. On December 3, day one of a week of services and seminars, M.L. stressed that the movement was about more than an end to segregation: "[T]he end is reconciliation; the end is redemption; the end is the creation of the beloved community." Equality of opportunity coupled with racial harmony was M.L.'s ultimate dream.

Montgomery didn't become a beloved community after bus desegregation. During the next few weeks, a white man who boarded a bus with only vacant seats in the back declared, "I would rather die and go to hell than sit behind a nigger"; a group of white men jumped a teenage black girl at a bus stop; a pregnant black woman suffered gunshot wounds to her legs; and several buses were shot at, as was M.L.'s home. There were six dynamite blasts on the night of January 10, 1957—four churches, two homes. On the hit list: the home of Robert Graetz, the white pastor of the largely black Lutheran congregation and a supporter of the boycott from day one. MIA cofounder Ralph Abernathy, the first friend M.L. made in Montgomery, was double-bombed: his home and his church (First Baptist). The two were together in Atlanta when Abernathy's wife, Juanita, telephoned about the night's reign of terror.

M.L. is about to take a symbolic ride aboard a city bus, now that segregated seating is history. Behind him is Reverend Glenn Smiley, of Fellowship of Reconciliation. He arrived in Montgomery in early 1956 to counsel M.L. on Gandhi and nonviolence.

At a mass meeting a few days later, as M.L. prayed, he said, "Lord, I hope no one will have to die as a result of our struggle for freedom in Montgomery. Certainly I don't want to die. But if anyone has to die, let it be me."

"No! No!" the crowd moaned.

M.L. just stood there, speechless, immobile, until led to his seat.

Two weeks later, dynamite wrecked the front of his home and a nearby taxi stand, sending three taxi drivers to the hospital with cuts from their shattered car windows. There would have been a second blast had the dozen sticks of dynamite on M.L.'s front porch detonated. There could have been more injuries or deaths had M.L. and his family been at home. His wife and daughter were in Atlanta. As for M.L., he had been at home earlier that evening, with Bob Williams, a friend since Morehouse who was working security. A few hours before the pre-dawn blast, something within prompted M.L. to get out of bed and wake his friend. "Bob, I think we better leave here tonight."

The cover story begins: "Across the South—in Atlanta, Mobile, Birmingham, Tallahassee, Miami, New Orleans—Negro leaders look toward Montgomery, Ala., the cradle of the Confederacy, for advice and counsel on how to gain the desegregation that the U.S. Supreme Court has guaranteed them. The man whose word they seek is not a judge, or a lawyer, or a political strategist or a flaming orator. He is a scholarly, 28-year-old Negro Baptist minister, the Rev. Martin Luther King Jr., who in little more than a year has risen from nowhere to become one of the nation's remarkable leaders of men."

TWENTY CENTS

FEBRUARY 18, 1957

TIME
THE WEEKLY NEWSMAGAZINE

Montgomery, Alabama's
REV. MARTIN LUTHER KING

$6.00 A YEAR

VOL. LXIX NO. 7

PART II

"I HOPE THOUSANDS WILL JOIN ME"

Montgomery made M.L. more than a man in the eyes of millions. The media made his name a household word, his face now recognized in near and distant lands. Many people went beyond admiration to adoration, turning M.L. into something he did not want to be: an idol. He worked hard to keep all the attention from going to his head. "Help me, O God, to see that I'm just a symbol of a movement," he prayed. "O God, help me to see that where I stand today, I stand because others helped me to stand there and because the forces of history projected me there. And this moment would have come in history even if M.L. King had never been born."

Also in 1957, M.L. spearheaded the formation of what became the Southern Christian Leadership Conference (SCLC), an umbrella group for church-based civil rights organizations. SCLC's motto: "To Redeem the Soul of America." Its first initiative was a black voter registration drive called the Crusade for Citizenship, which kicked off with simultaneous rallies in some twenty Southern cities on February 12, 1958, Abraham Lincoln's birthday. M.L. addressed the rally in Miami. Several days later, he was giving a speech at Mills College in Oakland, California. When he left California at month's end, he had fulfilled seven more engagements, in Asilomar, San Francisco, Los Angeles, and Pasadena.

Slow down, ease up, cut back, M.L.'s doctor advised in spring 1958. Press on, keep going, stay in motion, M.L. decided. His commitments included finishing his first book, *Stride Toward Freedom: The Montgomery Story*. While he was on a book tour, in September 1958, a deranged black woman, Izola Ware Curry, plunged a letter opener into his chest. "Don't prosecute her; get her healed," he told the police. After *he* healed, he heeded friends' advice that he visit the nation where Gandhi made history.

M.L.'s time in India (February 9 to March 10, 1959) included lectures and luncheons, dinner with Prime Minister Jawaharlal Nehru, and one-on-ones with disciples of Gandhi, as well as a stay at Gandhi's spartan Bombay home. At a shrine in New Delhi, M.L. paid homage to the Great Soul with prayer and flowers.

The poverty in India was inescapable. At times M.L. was depressed by the sight of seas of hunger-thin, homeless people. But on the whole, the trip was invigorating, spiritually. One majestic moment was a nature watch at the southern tip of India, at Cape Kanyakumari, where the Arabian Sea, Indian Ocean, and Bay of Bengal meet, and where some of Gandhi's ashes had been scattered. As M.L. and Coretta sat on a rock jutting out into the waters, they saw the setting of the sun in the west, then, in the east, the rising of the moon, a full moon. "I said to myself there is something in this that is an analogy to life," he told his congregation about a month later, in his Easter Sunday sermon. "So often we come to those points

**SEPTEMBER 20, 1958:
HARLEM,
NEW YORK CITY**

M.L. was autographing copies of *Stride Toward Freedom* in a department store when he was stabbed. "Everything is going to be all right," he calmly said. The woman tending to a cut on his hand knew better than to remove the letter opener from his chest. He later learned that had he sneezed or coughed he might have died. At nearby Harlem Hospital, extricating the blade, lodged between a lung and his heart, required removing part of his breastbone and two ribs. After surgery, M.L. developed pneumonia.

when it gets dark. It seems that the light of life is out . . . We get disillusioned and confused and give up in despair. But if we will only look around we will discover that God has another light." In that same sermon he recounted insights and inspirations that had seized him when he and his wife were in the Holy Land, one of the stops along the way in their journey home.

Once home, M.L. was on fire for SCLC to move boldly against segregation. But something had to give. Since the boycott, he had been shortchanging his church, being more figurehead than hands-on shepherd. Dexter deserved better than that, and SCLC deserved to have its leader living in Atlanta where it was headquartered (because the city was a transportation hub). In late November 1959, a tearful M.L. told his congregation that he was leaving. In stepping down from Dexter, he was not giving up pulpit ministry altogether. His father finally got

EBENEZER BAPTIST CHURCH: 407–413 AUBURN AVENUE, N.E., ATLANTA

The church was constructed (1914–1922) under the leadership of M.L.'s grandfather A.D. Williams.

APRIL 27, 1960:
563 JOHNSON AVENUE, ATLANTA

Little Marty looks on as his father removes a charred cross from the lawn of their home near Ebenezer. Burning crosses in front of people's homes, businesses, and houses of worship was a common KKK terror tactic. A few days before this cross burning, a bomb threat at Fisk University in Nashville delayed M.L.'s address there. In 1965, the Kings moved into a home on Sunset Avenue, in a working-class section of Atlanta.

his wish: M.L. became co-pastor of Ebenezer. His friend Ralph Abernathy also soon moved to Atlanta, becoming pastor of its West Hunter Street Baptist Church and shifting from SCLC's secretary-treasurer to its vice president.

M.L. hoped his return to Atlanta would mean more time "to meditate and think through the total struggle ahead," he remarked in a letter to graduate school professor turned friend Allan Chalmers. The times, however, kept M.L. on the move. He had speaking engagements here, there, almost everywhere to raise people's consciousness and dollars for SCLC. He had meetings in person and by telephone with advisers and colleagues on civil rights initiatives, such as demonstrations at the upcoming national conventions of the Democratic and Republican parties (in Los Angeles and Chicago, respectively). M.L. and his colleagues hoped to move both parties to add a meaningful civil rights plank to their election platforms.

In late June 1960, M.L. met with the man who would soon become the Democratic Party's presidential candidate, Massachusetts senator John Fitzgerald "Jack" Kennedy. M.L. left the meeting feeling that if Kennedy won the presidency, he would be an ally of the civil

THE GREENSBORO SIT-IN

On February 1, 1960, in Greensboro, North Carolina, several students at the state's Agricultural and Technical College bought a few items at Woolworth's, then sat down at its whites-only lunch counter and ordered coffee. The waitress refused to serve them; they refused to budge until the store closed. Their protest triggered more sit-ins at that Woolworth's and at lunch counters around the South, and in the North, sympathy pickets and boycotts of stores like Woolworth's, whose branches in the South discriminated against blacks. Lunch-counter sit-ins inspired read-ins at public libraries that banned blacks, wade-ins and swim-ins at whites-only public pools and beaches, and kneel-ins at churches. Many participants, most of whom were college students, were verbally and physically assaulted. If arrested, most refused to bail out before trial. This jail-no-bail stand was intended to draw more attention and sympathy to the cause. The lunch counter at the Woolworth's in Greensboro was opened to all people in July 1960.

rights movement. But it was a cautious optimism. He sized up Kennedy as "intel-lectually" committed, but felt this wealthy man lacked personal and "emotional involvement" with the cause.

By the time M.L. met with Kennedy, much of his energy had been spent contending with attempts to break him and sully his reputation. Shortly after he moved to Atlanta, he was charged with having cheated on his taxes when he lived in Montgomery. Though M.L. was found not guilty of tax fraud, the ordeal strained him. At times, he was tempted to call it quits, "to retreat to a more

The young activists planning sit-ins in Atlanta include two men surnamed King but of no relation to each other or M.L.: far to M.L.'s right, Lonnie King, cofounder of the Committee on Appeal for Human Rights. Next to him, Ed King, the Student Nonviolent Coordinating Committee's executive secretary. To M.L.'s left, Carolyn Banks. Next to her, Julian Bond, a Morehouse Man, SNCC's communications director, and a future politician.

quiet and serene life," he admitted in a piece for *Christian Century* magazine. "But every time such a temptation appeared, something came to strengthen and sustain my determination." The sit-in movement was part of that something.

While some black leaders denounced the sit-ins, M.L. praised them. On April 15, 1960, he delivered the keynote speech at the founding conference of SNCC (pronounced *snick*), the organization born of the sit-in movement. In his address, M.L. implored the young activists to set their sights on more than the "Promised Land," a metaphor for racial justice. "Our ultimate end must be the creation of the beloved community," he stressed, just as he had done four years earlier in Montgomery.

M.L. watched with hope, with wonder, while the sit-in movement took root in Atlanta, making time to meet with its leaders—in his home, at Ebenezer, even at the airport before boarding a flight. He eventually gave in to their plea to join them in sit-ins at eateries in Atlanta's largest department store, Rich's.

> For the first time in his life, M.L. spent a night behind bars.

"I had to practice what I preached," M.L. told a reporter inside a Fulton County jail on the afternoon of Wednesday, October 19, 1960, following the sit-in at Rich's. For the first time in his life, M.L. spent a night behind bars. Along with dozens of other protesters, he held fast to the jail-no-bail stance until the charges—trespassing—were dropped and desegregation talks were on the table. M.L. rejoiced when Rich's conceded a few days later. But by participating in the sit-in, he had triggered trouble from another county.

Several months back, while driving the writer Lillian Smith from Atlanta to a hospital in DeKalb County, Georgia, for her cancer treatment, M.L. had been ticketed for not having a Georgia driver's license within ninety days of relocation to that state, as the law required. The police probably never would have pulled him over had he and Coretta not been in the car with a white woman at a time and in a place where blacks and whites doing anything together as equals—even just riding in a car—rankled many whites.

WALKING THE WALK

Soon after his arrest for trying to have a meal at Rich's Magnolia Room, M.L. stood before a judge, explaining that he and his young friends had sought to "bring the whole issue of racial injustice under the scrutiny of the conscience of Atlanta. I must honestly say that we firmly believe that segregation is evil, and that our Southland will never reach its full potential and moral maturity until this cankerous disease is removed. We do not seek to remove this unjust system for ourselves alone but for our white brothers as well. The festering sore of segregation debilitates the white man as well as the Negro."

M.L. thought his traffic violation was resolved with his payment of a twenty-five-dollar fine, unaware that he was on probation for twelve months. Authorities in DeKalb County seized upon his arrest at Rich's as a probation violation and wanted him turned over to them. The students wanted to stand by M.L. by staying in jail until he was released, but he urged them not to do that, as did his father. "M.L. will be all right," he said.

M.L. was not all right on October 25 when taken to his hearing at the DeKalb County courthouse, where a judge sentenced him to four months' hard labor. He was not all right when his sister, then his wife, pregnant with their third child, burst into tears. His father and brother were also on hand for moral support.

"Corrie, dear, you have to be strong," he told his wife when she and his father were allowed to see him in the court's holding cell after the sentencing.

M.L. himself later struggled to be strong in the DeKalb County jail, sharing a cell with several other men, sleep his only relief. Sleep was brief, however. Before dawn he was awakened by a flashlight's blinding beam and a jailer's bark: "King, get up!"

[**M.L. himself later struggled to be strong in the DeKalb County jail, sharing a cell with several other men, sleep his only relief.**]

He had no idea where he was being taken when he was hustled into a car in shackles. During a seemingly endless ride through autumnal darkness, he wondered if he'd see tomorrow.

Around daybreak, the sheriff's car pulled up to the maximum-security prison in Reidsville, Georgia.

The cockroaches in his cell were legion, the food rancid. The thought of being on a chain gang—forced to do backbreaking construction work, shackled to hardened criminals—was more than he could bear. He broke down; he wept.

He also wrote his wife. "I urge you to be strong in the faith, and this will in turn strengthen me." He told her that he was "asking God hourly" for "the power of endurance," and believing "that this excessive suffering that is now coming to our family will in some little way serve to make Atlanta a better city, Georgia a better state, and America a better country. Just how I do not yet know, but I have faith to believe it will." Meanwhile, Sunday was visiting day at Reidsville. "I know it will be a terrible inconvenience in your condition, but I want to see you and the children very badly." He asked her to bring a radio, a Bible, a book on Gandhi,

J. Wallace Hamilton's *Horns and Halos in Human Nature*, a copy of *Stride Toward Freedom*, and "my reference dictionary called *Increasing Your Word Power*."

His wife didn't have to make the trip to Reidsville. M.L. was released the next day. He soon found out that Jack Kennedy had telephoned Coretta and pledged to help, then his right-hand man, brother Bobby, had placed a call to the judge who had sentenced M.L. The surge of blacks casting their votes for Jack Kennedy two weeks later contributed to his slim margin of victory when he won the presidency.

OCTOBER 27, 1960: FREE AT LAST

The crowd celebrating M.L.'s release from Reidsville includes Coretta, his sister, Christine (facing the camera), and his children, Yoki and Marty.

As M.L. looked ahead to a new year—one that would bring him and Coretta a second son, Dexter—he did so yearning for President Kennedy to make a bold stand for racial justice. That yearning intensified in spring 1961 with the advent of the Freedom Rides initiated by the Congress for Racial Equality (CORE): the sojourns of selfless souls into the South to challenge segregation in interstate transportation facilities, from waiting rooms to ticket windows and lunch counters. The Supreme Court had outlawed this facet of Jim Crow in 1960, but many Southern localities continued to maintain it. The attacks on Freedom Riders compelled the Kennedy administration to pressure the Interstate Commerce Commission (ICC) to take action. In late September 1961, the ICC issued a ruling that forbade interstate carriers to use terminals that segregated. "Colored" and "White" signs had to come down. Terminals that didn't comply—and the lunch counters and other businesses within them—would end up out of business. The ruling went into effect November 1.

MAY 14, 1961:
OUTSIDE ANNISTON, ALABAMA

When this Greyhound bus carrying Freedom Riders pulled into the bus terminal in Anniston, whites surrounded it, some bearing lead pipes, baseball bats, and bicycle chains. The mob slashed tires and smashed windows. When the bus departed, about fifty cars and pickup trucks gave chase.

**SUNDAY, MAY 21, 1961:
FIRST BAPTIST CHURCH,
MONTGOMERY**

About 1,500 people had poured into the church Reverend Abernathy once pastored to pay tribute to and hear testimony from a group of Freedom Riders who had survived mob violence at Montgomery's bus depot. (One of their comrades, and a Justice Department official traveling with them, had been beaten unconscious.) By evening, several thousand whites surrounded First Baptist, pelting it with rocks and tear gas bombs, and threatening arson. M.L. had flown in from Chicago earlier that day. He urged the people trapped in First Baptist to keep the faith. At turns, he was on the phone with Bobby Kennedy (by then the U.S. attorney general) heatedly pleading for help, concerned that the marshals on the scene would not suffice to keep the mob at bay.

TRAPPED IN FIRST BAPTIST

Thanks to Bobby Kennedy's intervention, around 6 A.M. on Monday, May 22, members of the National Guard began escorting people home. Violence and the threat of violence didn't stop the Freedom Rides. Hundreds of people volunteered for Freedom Rides in the summer of 1961. Participants ranged from college students and professors to rabbis and Christian clerics. Along with violence, many endured jail—more than three hundred people in Mississippi alone.

Some members of SNCC were disappointed in M.L. for not going on a Freedom Ride. "I think I should choose the time and place of my Golgotha," he snapped in response to them. They were shocked by his reference to himself and the site of Jesus' crucifixion in the same breath.

In contrast, M.L. didn't hesitate to get involved with goings-on two hundred miles southwest of Atlanta, in Albany, Georgia, where SNCC workers had launched a voter registration drive and workshops in nonviolence. Added to that, local high school and college students as well as out-of-towners had been arrested when they tried to exercise their right to be in any part of the bus and train stations. By early December, about five hundred people had endured arrest, most for participating in marches and prayer vigils at City Hall in support of the young bravehearts. The organization in charge of the action was called the Albany Movement, a coalition of several organizations, including the Albany Federation of Colored Women's Clubs, the NAACP Youth Council, and SNCC.

> By early December, about five hundred people had endured arrest, most for participating in marches and prayer vigils.

To drum up more moral and financial support for their cause, the Albany Movement's president, osteopath William Anderson, reached out to M.L. All Anderson asked was that he speak at one rally. Some of Anderson's colleagues didn't even want M.L. to do that. They feared that his presence would turn local leadership into lesser lights. M.L. was unaware of this resentment when he arrived in Albany in mid-December. The people who came with him included Ralph Abernathy and SCLC executive director Reverend Wyatt Tee Walker.

Freedom songs were in the air as M.L. approached Albany's Shiloh Baptist Church, the main site of the rally. The overflow crowd was in a church across the street. Loudspeakers kept the two bodies of people in communion.

PRAYERFUL

Jim Crow was absolute in Albany, where blacks were more than 30 percent of the population.

M.L. tapped his precious themes—exalting justice and *agape*, extolling sacrifice and suffering for a righteous cause. When he finished, the church broke into a powerful rendition of the era's top civil rights anthem, "We Shall Overcome." Caught up in the soul-force pulsing through the people, Anderson called for a march the next day. When asked to lead it, M.L., just as caught up, said yes.

Around four o'clock the following afternoon, under an Albany sky aching rain, M.L. and Anderson stepped from Shiloh arm in arm. Behind them was

Abernathy arm in arm with Mrs. Anderson. Two hundred-plus people followed, two by two. As the procession passed through the city's black main street, with its grocery stores, pool halls, and barbershops, only a few bystanders joined the march. Most folks just stared. Farther along, closer to City Hall, a sea of yellow-slickered lawmen awaited the marchers. Anderson saluted several police officers with "God bless you."

"Do you have a written permit to parade or demonstrate?" Police Chief Laurie Pritchett asked M.L.

"We are simply going to pray at City Hall."

Chief Pritchett simply had M.L. and others taken to various jails.

M.L., with Abernathy and Anderson, landed in a jail in Americus, Georgia, about thirty-five miles south of Albany. Abernathy quickly bonded out so that he could talk to the media and in other ways raise support for the movement in Albany. Wyatt Walker (not arrested) did likewise, issuing press releases and making brassy statements about SCLC's readiness to do its utmost for the Albany campaign. Walker's ways reinforced some Albany Movement members' fear of an SCLC takeover. Resentment reached high tide when word spread of what M.L. told reporters after he refused to be bailed out: "If convicted, I will refuse to pay the fine. I expect to spend Christmas in jail. I hope thousands will join me." That didn't happen. He spent Christmas with his family.

He bonded out on December 18, after an Albany Movement officer negotiated a truce with city officials. The Albany Movement agreed to cease demonstrations because the city agreed to assemble a biracial committee to discuss black demands in January and to the bail-free release of roughly seven hundred Albany Movement people in jail. M.L. was out of the loop on this hasty deal. It was pretty obvious that there were blacks in Albany who wanted M.L. out of the spotlight as much as most whites did. One newspaper declared M.L.'s engagement with the Albany campaign "a devastating loss of face" for him. However, M.L. kept envisioning victory. He knew he would have to return to Albany to stand trial for that December arrest. He expected to be found guilty and was prepared to do jail time.

By the time he and Abernathy returned a few months later for their court date, city officials had failed to assemble the biracial committee. Tensions were high because of this and because the Albany Movement had launched a bus boycott in reaction to the arrest of Ola Mae Quarterman, a student at Albany State College (now University). Ola Mae had landed in jail in mid-January for disorderly conduct because she had sat in the front of a city bus, and when asked to move, told the driver, "I paid my damn twenty cents, and I can sit where I want." Within weeks the bus company suspended operations, so successful was the boycott.

When M.L. and Abernathy were found guilty on February 27, 1962, the judge postponed sentencing for sixty days. That sixty days became four months. When they were finally sentenced on

["I paid my damn twenty cents, and I can sit where I want."]

July 10, the judge gave them a choice of a fine of $178 or jail time of forty-five days. They chose jail. But forty-five days became two. On July 12, Chief Pritchett released them. He claimed that some black man had plunked down $356 in cash for their fines. M.L. and Abernathy protested, because they had not authorized anyone to do that. Too bad. With their fines paid, they had to leave jail. M.L. didn't know who paid his fine, but he knew it was a ruse to diffuse and confuse the movement. (A local white lawyer, in cahoots with city officials, had in fact paid the fines.)

Shortly after his release, M.L. aimed to "turn Albany upside down." He called for yet another march, in about a week. But once again his plans were stymied. City officials got a federal judge to issue an injunction against the march. This restraining order prohibited M.L. and other Albany Movement leaders from

SOUL-FORCE

Chief Pritchett had studied up on M.L. and was intent on outsmarting him by denying him any kind of confrontation that would make front-page news. He ordered his men to be courteous to demonstrators. Beatings of Albany activists in jails and elsewhere received little or no press.

even encouraging a demonstration, let alone leading one. They received notice of the court order on the morning of the scheduled march, Saturday, July 21.

In the ensuing powwow at Anderson's house, some Albany Movement members urged defiance of the injunction, others obedience. Bobby Kennedy and Burke Marshall, head of the Justice Department's civil rights division, pressed for compliance with the injunction. When M.L. conferred with them by telephone, they stressed what M.L. knew well: that the federal government was black people's best hope for the righting of civil rights wrongs. The *Brown* decision and the ICC ruling were just two examples. What's more, one of the ways segregationists maintained segregation was by defying federal laws. If M.L. did likewise, he could lose the moral high ground, not to mention whatever favor he had with the Kennedy administration.

As the debate about whether to march went on, there were folks at Shiloh with their marching shoes on. Sam Wells, pastor of a small church out in the country, was kindling their courage with his passionate preaching between rounds of singing. When word reached Wells that M.L. and Albany Movement chiefs had arrived and were in the pastor's study, he made a beeline for that room and told M.L., "Dr. King, the world is waiting for a message. They are looking and listening for a message tonight." M.L. had made up his mind not to march and to have lawyers appeal to a higher court, but he had not decided what to say to the people waiting to march.

When Wells returned to the pulpit, he took matters into his own hands. He became the message. "I've heard about an injunction, but I haven't seen one! I heard a few names, but my name hasn't been called! But I do know where my name *is* being called. My name is being called on the road to freedom . . . We will go down to the City Hall and we will protest peacefully the evils that have been grinding the life out of our spirits for ninety-nine years." About two hundred people followed him and ended up under arrest. When M.L. heard of Wells's maverick move, he was so pleased: "They can stop the leaders, but they can't stop the people."

Three days later, the injunction was quashed on appeal. M.L. and Anderson immediately sent a message to Albany's Mayor Kelley requesting a meeting to discuss black grievances. There were to be no more protests while they awaited the mayor's response. But M.L. and Anderson couldn't stop the people—people fired up over the assault on physical therapist Marion King, wife of the Albany Movement's vice president, Slater King (no relation to M.L.).

BEHIND THE SCENES DURING THE ALBANY CAMPAIGN

The people in this planning session include: Jean Young, left, wife of Congregational minister Andrew "Andy" Young, SCLC senior staffer since summer 1961; Wyatt Walker (on the phone), SCLC's executive director, whose prior activism included spearheading protests for school desegregation in Petersburg, Virginia, where he was pastor of the Gillfield Baptist Church; and Coretta, center. The man seated to Coretta's left is Henry Schwarzschild of the American Civil Liberties Union. They are working in Dr. Anderson's home.

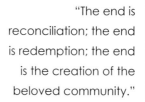

"The end is reconciliation; the end is redemption; the end is the creation of the beloved community."

PART III

"I'VE GOT TO MARCH"

Nothing could tear M.L. away from the movement. Not defeat in Albany. Not the lure of a guaranteed annual income of $100,000 from a speakers bureau. Not the fact that he and Coretta had a fourth child on the way (daughter Bernice). Not nonstop death threats. Not a pummeling from a burly neo-Nazi, Roy James, during an address. M.L. made no attempt at self-defense. At one point, he even lowered his hands from his face. "I'm not interested in pressing charges," he later said. "I'm interested in changing the kind of system that produces this kind of man." *Agape* and his hope for the beloved community still held sway, even with a swollen jaw and bruised back.

That attack happened in September 1962 at an SCLC convention in the Alabama steel town of Birmingham, where Commissioner of Public Safety Eugene "Bull" Conner had blared that blood would "run in the streets" before the city desegregated, where dynamite blasts had rocked black churches and homes, where Reverend Fred Shuttlesworth had spearheaded a boycott of stores, and where M.L.'s brother, A.D., pastored a church. There, in this city with the sad sobriquet "Bombingham," M.L. next lent his might to a campaign for the Promised Land. The primary targets were the city's downtown stores with their whites-only lunch counters and no-blacks policies when it came to hiring clerks.

AT HOME

Like most couples, M.L. and Coretta had their ups and downs.

"Segregation now! Segregation tomorrow! Segregation forever!" proclaimed Alabama governor George Wallace in his January 1963 inaugural address. *Freedom Now!* vowed Birmingham blacks, who staged sit-ins and pickets in early April. M.L. was set to lead a major march on April 12, which was also Good Friday, but the day before, he and key comrades were slapped with a court order forbidding them to march. Making matters worse, the campaign had run out of money for bailing out hundreds of people still in jail from the first wave of protests.

> "I don't know where the money will come from, but I have to make a faith act," he said. "I've got so many people depending upon me, I've got to march."

On Good Friday morning, M.L. huddled with two dozen colleagues in the Gaston Motel's room 30, the suite that served as his command center. Abernathy, Shuttlesworth, Walker, and Andy Young were there, as was M.L.'s father. He was among those pressing M.L. to forget the march and focus on fundraising.

As the debate became more than M.L. could stand, he stepped away into another room for solitude. When he emerged, he had exchanged his trousers for blue jeans and put a denim work shirt over his white dress shirt. "I don't know where the money will come from, but I have to make a faith act," he said. "I've got so many people depending upon me, I've got to march." His father objected, but dissent soon dissolved. The men joined hands, then joined voices in "We Shall Overcome."

Later that day, M.L. was locked away in solitary confinement, lying on a cot that was not a cot—no mattress, blanket, or pillow—just bedsprings. He spent hour after hour in almost total darkness. Finally, on Easter Sunday, two of his lawyers were allowed to see him. The next day, another attorney came bearing

GOOD FRIDAY, 1963

When middle-class people like M.L. and Abernathy wore denim, they were not making a fashion statement, but a political one: expressing solidarity with the poor, many of whom wore denim pants, shirts, and overalls on a regular basis because they were cheap and durable.

very good tidings: Entertainer Harry Belafonte had raised fifty thousand dollars for the Birmingham campaign. "I don't know whether the sun was shining at that moment," M.L. later wrote. "But I know that once again I could see the light."

FRED SHUTTLESWORTH

Shuttlesworth founded the Alabama Christian Movement for Human Rights and cofounded SCLC. He's seen here after KKK members bombed his home on Christmas night 1956. At the time, Shuttlesworth was pastor of Birmingham's Bethel Baptist Church. In September 1957, he suffered a vicious beating, and his wife, Ruby, suffered a stabbing from a white mob as they tried to enroll two of their children in a "white" school.

M.L. also began to see scraps of mercy from his jailers: bedding, a chance to shower, a call to his wife. She had telephoned Bobby Kennedy, worried about her husband's well–being, his life. In response, the Kennedy administration pressured

Birmingham officials to ease up a little on M.L. In the meantime, eight white Alabama clerics had come down on him hard. He learned this when one of his lawyers slipped him a recent issue of the *Birmingham News*. In it, an open letter from a rabbi, a Roman Catholic bishop, and six Protestant ministers calling the Birmingham campaign "unwise and untimely," and its "extreme measures" unnecessary. They never mentioned M.L. by name, but it was clear that he was the main target of their reprimand—an outsider who should leave Birmingham business to Birmingham people. Righteous rage roused M.L. to respond.

What began as scribbles in the margins of the newspaper, jottings on toilet paper, and lines of prose on note paper surged into the roughly seven-thousand-word "Letter from Birmingham Jail." Addressed to the eight clerics, the letter was meant for the nation, the world. In it, he dealt with the charge that what went on in Birmingham was none of his business: "I cannot sit idly by in Atlanta and not be concerned about what happens in Birmingham. Injustice anywhere is a threat to justice everywhere." He rejected the notion that blacks

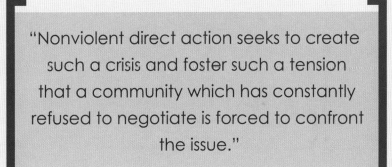

"Nonviolent direct action seeks to create such a crisis and foster such a tension that a community which has constantly refused to negotiate is forced to confront the issue."

should rely more on dialogue than on demonstrations: "Nonviolent direct action seeks to create such a crisis and foster such a tension that a community which has constantly refused to negotiate is forced to confront the issue. It seeks so to dramatize the issue that it can no longer be ignored." He stressed that blacks had "not made a single gain in civil rights without determined legal and nonviolent pressure."

M.L. rebuked the eight clerics and their ilk for suggesting that blacks were in too much of a hurry for their rights and ought to exercise more patience. He spoke not only for and of himself, but for and of millions of his people, living and dead:

We have waited for more than 340 years for our constitutional and God-given rights . . . Perhaps it is easy for those who have never felt the stinging darts of segregation to say, "Wait." But when you have seen vicious mobs lynch your mothers and fathers at will and drown your sisters and brothers at whim; when you have seen hate-filled policemen curse, kick and even kill your black brothers and sisters; when you see the vast majority of your twenty million Negro brothers smothering in an airtight cage of poverty in the midst of an affluent society; when you suddenly find your tongue twisted and your speech stammering as you seek to explain to your six-year-old daughter why she can't go to the public amusement park that has just been advertised on television, and see tears welling up in her eyes when she is told that Funtown is closed to colored children, and see ominous clouds of inferiority beginning to form in her little mental sky, and see her beginning to distort her personality by developing an unconscious bitterness toward white people; when you have to concoct an answer for a five-year-old son who is asking: "Daddy, why do white people treat colored people so mean?" . . . when you are humiliated day in and day out by nagging signs reading "white" and "colored" . . . when you are harried by day and haunted by night by the fact that you are a Negro, living constantly at tiptoe stance, never quite knowing what to expect next . . . when you are forever fighting a degenerating sense of "nobodiness"—then you will understand why we find it difficult to wait.

M.L. lamented in his letter that so many white clerics—people who claimed a hunger for the holy—were not blazingly impatient for racial justice. He recalled the numerous times during travels around the Southland that he passed by whites-only houses of worship and wondered, "What kind of people worship here? Who is their God?"

IN BIRMINGHAM JAIL

On April 20, M.L. bonded out of jail at the urging of his attorneys. They wanted quality time with him before his upcoming trial. Found guilty, he remained out on bail while his lawyers appealed his case, which he ended up losing. In November 1967, he returned to Birmingham to serve a five-day sentence. This photo was taken then.

While M.L. was in jail, practically all the men and women primed for protest were behind bars. Again, he faced the prospect of a failed campaign. Then, one of his lieutenants, Jim Bevel, came up with an idea some considered godforsaken. The children. Birmingham had thousands of black children. Let the children join the crusade, Bevel urged.

Out of Sixteenth Street Baptist Church, day after May day, girls and boys, some six, some sixteen, devoted their feet, their voices, their courage to the cause despite water cannons, billy clubs, gun butts, and snarling dogs.

"It makes me sick," said President Kennedy of the police brutality. Scenes from Birmingham, flashed on television, splashed across newspapers, disgusted others across the nation, around the world. America was embarrassed. Birmingham could not be ignored. Plans for desegregation and the meeting of other demands were hammered out on Friday, May 10, 1963.

Mourning replaced M.L.'s joy the following night. Birmingham was

WATER-WHIPPED IN BIRMINGHAM

The sight of cops abusing children impelled many adults to join the protests.

LONGING FOR THE PROMISED LAND

Several thousand young people took part in Birmingham's "Children's Crusade." With the jails full, authorities held some of them in a sports stadium. Before joining in the demonstrations, youngsters had to get permission from a parent or guardian. Like adult demonstrators, they also had to sign a pledge that they would abide by the campaign's ten commandments. They included "Meditate daily on the life and teachings of Jesus," "Walk and talk in the manner of love, for God is love," and "Refrain from violence of fist, tongue and heart."

Bombingham again. His brother's home was hit, but thankfully, A.D., his wife, and their children suffered no physical injuries. Another blast wrecked the area around room 30 of the Gaston Motel. The culprits were, no doubt, unaware that M.L. had returned to Atlanta. He rushed back to Birmingham to comfort his brother and to call for calm in the black community, for some had responded to the bombings with rioting. M.L. struggled not to despair.

FACING THE NATION

In his televised address, President Kennedy acknowledged that although slavery had ended long ago, black Americans were still not truly free. "They are not yet freed from the bonds of injustice; they are not yet freed from social and economic oppression. And this nation, for all its hopes and all its boasts, will not be fully free until all its citizens are free."

About a month after the bombings, on the evening of June 11, 1963, President Kennedy announced that he was sending Congress a bill that would abolish segregation in public facilities—from pools to parks, restrooms to restaurants. "We are confronted primarily with a moral issue. It is as old as the scriptures and is as clear as the American Constitution," the president said. He cited the Birmingham campaign among the recent events that had "so increased the cries for equality that no city or state or legislative body can prudently choose to ignore them."

To keep the freedom cries from being ignored, SCLC had joined with CORE, SNCC, the NAACP, and other organizations in mounting a monumental march to the nation's capital—the march that became the era's march of marches, where M.L. delivered his best-known speech, an overflow of his hallowed hope for an America that would make the angels sing.

**AUGUST 28, 1963:
THE MARCH ON
WASHINGTON FOR
JOBS AND FREEDOM**

About a quarter-million people attended the march, in the centennial year of the Emancipation Proclamation, making it the largest demonstration in America as of that date. "They came from almost every state of the union; they came in every form of transportation; they gave up from one to three days pay plus the cost of transportation, which for many was a heavy financial sacrifice," M.L. recalled in his book *Why We Can't Wait.* "They applauded their leaders generously, but the leaders, in their hearts, applauded their audience." Those leaders included A. Philip Randolph, the event's masterbuilder. M.L. called the crowd "an army without guns, but not without strength . . . It was a fighting army, but no one could mistake that its most powerful weapon was love."

"I HAVE A DREAM"

M.L. was midway through his prepared remarks when he went off script and shifted from giving a speech to preaching. From the dais, gospel great Mahalia Jackson urged, "Tell them about your dream, Martin! Tell them about the dream!" M.L. reached into memory for the "I have a dream" refrain he had used on other occasions.

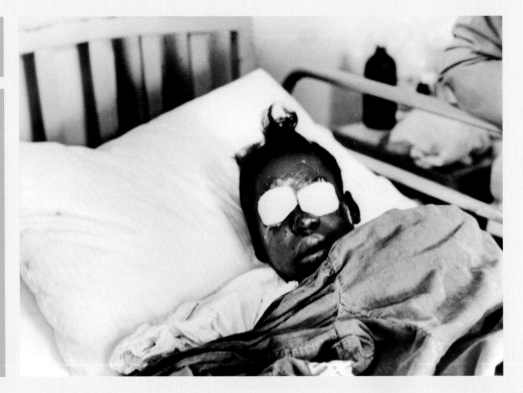

WOUNDED IN THE HOUSE OF THE LORD

Twelve-year-old Sarah Jean Collins was among those injured in the Sunday, September 15, 1963, bombing of Sixteenth Street Baptist Church. She ended up losing her right eye. Her fourteen-year-old sister was one of the four girls who lost their lives in the blast, the work of the KKK.

About two weeks after the mountaintop experience of the March on Washington, M.L. wondered if he was just a fool dreamer. *Was it all worth it?* he asked himself, as he absorbed bad news yet again out of Bombingham: an attack on Sixteenth Street Baptist Church. M.L. strove to do what he soon entreated others to do in his eulogy for victims of the bombing: believe that "God still has a way of wringing good out of evil."

Before the end of 1963, he was in grief's grip again, as was most of the nation. In the early afternoon of November 22, M.L. was at home getting ready to head out of town for yet another fundraiser, when his television flashed a bulletin: President Kennedy had been shot while in Dallas. M.L. and Coretta were still glued to the television about an hour later, when word went out that the president was dead.

"This is what is going to happen to me also," M.L. said to Coretta. "I keep telling you this is a sick society."

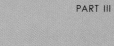

Reverends Shuttlesworth and Abernathy follow M.L. into Sixth Avenue Baptist Church for the funeral of Addie Mae Collins, Carol Denise McNair, and Cynthia Diane Wesley. The parents of the fourth victim, Carole Robertson, had a separate funeral for her.

Like all souls tried and tested and cleaving to a sacred commitment, M.L. knew that agonies often follow ecstasies, as valleys follow mountain peaks. Denial of this reality could result in whiplash of the soul and spiritual paralysis. To stay in motion, in the movement, and in his right mind, he had to rely on more than publicity and plans. Staying power meant staying prayerful.

Prayerful: When the January 3, 1964, issue of *Time* magazine named him "Man of the Year."

Prayerful: When the spring campaign against segregation in KKK-infested St. Augustine, Florida, and his three days in jail (for a restaurant sit-in) ended with no Jim-Crow-crashing change, only battered black bodies.

Prayerful: When SNCC worker Bob Moses masterminded "Freedom Summer," mobilizing hundreds of Northerners, the majority white, to join Southern civil rights activists in Mississippi.

Prayerful: When news broke that three Freedom Summer soldiers had disappeared—Jim Chaney, Andy Goodman, Mickey Schwerner. Last seen in Philadelphia, Mississippi. Last seen in the hands of police.

Prayerful: When President Lyndon Baines Johnson signed his predecessor's civil rights bill into law in July 1964.

Prayerful: When, later that summer, some blacks in New York City, Chicago, and elsewhere in the North said, "No!" to nonviolent protest and rioted in reaction to police brutality, stifled opportunities, and hope-starved lives.

Prayerful: When he received the preeminent prize for apostles of peace.

When M.L. found out about the Nobel Peace Prize in October 1964, he was in an Atlanta hospital overcoming exhaustion. Two months later, in his acceptance speech at Norway's Oslo University, he spoke of his "audacious faith in the future of mankind" and his belief that "peoples everywhere can have three meals a day for their bodies, education and culture for their minds, and dignity, equality, and freedom for their spirits." He gave away the $54,000 that came with the prize to six organizations, CORE, the NAACP, SCLC, and SNCC among them.

JULY 2, 1964:
THE WHITE HOUSE
(EAST ROOM)

President Lyndon Johnson shakes M.L.'s hand after signing the Civil Rights Act of 1964, designed to combat discrimination in public accommodation, employment, and other arenas against an array of people, not just blacks. In his State of the Union address earlier in the year, Johnson had called for a "War on Poverty." Several months later, he outlined his vision of America as a "Great Society": one that "demands an end to poverty and racial injustice," for starters. In August, he signed the Economic Opportunity Act, the cradle of anti-poverty initiatives such as Head Start, Neighborhood Youth Corps, and Work-Study for college students.

As a Nobel laureate, M.L. could have shifted into the kind of spiritual leader who issues directives and inspiration from some Edenic estate. College president? He could have taken any number of well-paying jobs, pursued a course less stressful and dangerous than crusading for social justice, but M.L. kept treading the stony road.

**FEBRUARY 1, 1965:
READY TO REGISTER
IN SELMA**

They are on their way to the courthouse in Selma, Alabama, seat of Dallas County, where only about 20 percent of blacks eligible to vote were registered. This march will result in M.L. spending five days in jail. A few weeks earlier, as he registered at a whites-only hotel in Selma, a white man jumped him, with a white woman cheering, "Get him! Get him!" On Sunday, March 7, came massive violence: As several hundred people undertook a fifty-mile march from Selma to the state capitol building in Montgomery, lawmen set upon them with billy clubs, bullwhips, cattle prods, and tear gas. "Bloody Sunday" inspired an upsurge of support for a vigorous voting rights bill. M.L. was in Atlanta on that day.

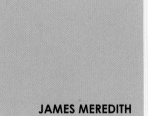

JAMES MEREDITH

Meredith, who had integrated the University of Mississippi at Oxford in 1962, was shot on Highway 51 near Hernando, Mississippi, on June 7, 1966. As Meredith lay in the hospital, M.L. and other activists pledged to pick up the march where Meredith was shot. Meredith's walk from Memphis, Tennessee, to Jackson, the capital of Mississippi, became the Meredith March. M.L. was not with the two-hundred-plus-mile march continuously.

M.L. stayed on the stony road with the Selma voting rights campaign—a catalyst for the 1965 Voting Rights Act, which outlawed literacy tests and other voter registration impediments and resulted in a quarter-million new black voters on the rolls within months of its passage.

He also put his life on the line in riot-ripped Watts, in August 1965, walking through that section of Los Angeles preaching peace to seething blacks, one of whom told him, "Go back where you came from!"

M.L. didn't dodge danger a year later, in Mississippi, after Air Force veteran James Meredith was gunned down on day two of his "walk against fear," his personal protest against violence heaped on civil rights crusaders.

From afar, M.L. seemed fearless. Exuding calm in public was one of his many gifts. (And we often forget that courage is not the absence of fear, but fortitude in the face of fear.)

M.L. was clearly fearful during the Meredith March, especially when he headed up a pilgrimage to Philadelphia, Mississippi, on the second anniversary of the murders of Chaney, Goodman, and Schwerner, whose bullet-ridden bodies had been found buried beneath a dam outside the city. As M.L. and about two hundred people marched from Mount Nebo Baptist Church to the city's downtown, bystanders hurled insults, a car or two careened within inches of them, and a man tried to club backs and heads from inside a pickup truck. Still, M.L. marched.

There was a prayer service in front of the jail where the three civil rights workers had been detained, then a memorial service near the county courthouse. At points M.L. couldn't be heard, so loud was the shout-down from a crowd of about three hundred whites. The tremble in M.L.'s voice wasn't from a quickening of the Holy Spirit, but from fear. As he tried to inspire his followers with fortitude, he said, "I believe in my heart that the murderers are somewhere around me at this moment."

"You're damn right, they're right behind you right now," muttered a man later imprisoned for his role in the killings, Deputy Sheriff Cecil Price, a member of the KKK. M.L. froze, cut his speech short, and handed off to Reverend Abernathy for the closing prayer.

M.L. couldn't shake the feeling that he would be killed in Mississippi. Still, he marched. Despite the physical attack on the procession as they returned to Mount Nebo. Despite state troopers' tear-gassing and billy-club-bashing frenzy two days later in Canton, Mississippi, as he tried to hold a rally on the grounds of a black school. Still, M.L. marched. And when the march reached Jackson on June 26, 1966, climaxing with a rally attended by about fifteen thousand people, a very drained M.L. delivered a lackluster speech.

BLACK POWER!

In mid-June 1966, during the Meredith March, SNCC's recently elected new chair, Stokely Carmichael (mike in hand), addressed a rally in Greenwood, Mississippi, after his arrest for trying to put up tents for marchers on the grounds of a school. "This is the twenty-seventh time I have been arrested—and I ain't going to jail no more!" he declared. "The only way we gonna stop them white men from whuppin' us is to take over. We been saying freedom for six years and we ain't got nothin'. What we gonna start saying now is Black Power!" Soon Carmichael and the crowd had a call and response going on: "What do you want?" he cried out. "Black Power!" people shouted back. "What do you want?" . . . "Black Power!" Carmichael (later named Kwame Toure) had been a Freedom Rider in 1961, for which he spent more than forty days in notoriously brutal Parchman Prison (Parchman, Mississippi). Carmichael had also done voter registration work in Mississippi. In Lowndes County, Alabama, he had helped organize an all-black political party, which took a growling black panther as its logo.

Being in Mississippi, feeling in the valley of the shadow of death—more than that had M.L. downcast. Along the way, he had contended with what he deemed a destructive spirit on the rise among some with whom he marched. Younger blacks bristled at the presence of whites in the march—in the movement, period. They were tired of turn-the-other-cheek tactics. They wanted to go Old Testament: an eye for an eye, a tooth for a tooth. Rejecting prayer power, their rallying cry was "Black Power!" They were in a place he had forsaken so long ago. *How could I love a race of people who hated me? Agape*'s appeal was slipping away.

M.L. stayed his course. What's more, he was determined to enlarge his mission field: to challenge de facto segregation and spotlight blighted black lives in the North. He did this in Chicago, where police brutality was rife and many blacks had limited job opportunities and lousy housing. To right these wrongs, the Chicago Freedom Movement was organized, a joint effort between SCLC and the city's Coordinating Council of Community Organizations.

IN "SLUMDALE"

To draw attention to the plight of many black Chicagoans, M.L. rented a third-floor walk-up in a predominantly black West Side neighborhood, North Lawndale. The ratty two-bedroom apartment cost ninety dollars a month, whereas a larger, nicer apartment in a whites-only neighborhood rented for about ten dollars less. During the summer of 1966, Coretta and the kids were with M.L. much of the time that he lived in the Chicago apartment. In this photo, taken in February 1966, the couple helps fix up a nearby building.

In Chicago, M.L. led a Sunday rally at Soldier Field and afterward affixed demands to the doors of City Hall. He rushed out into the streets urging calm when it seemed that riots would consume the West Side after police officers turned off fire hydrants that black youngsters had turned to for relief from dog-day heat. M.L. also engaged in long, intense hours of talk with the city's formidable mayor, Richard J. Daley, and ministered to gang members, teaching them, pleading with them to pursue the nonviolent path.

"We want King! We want King!" whites chanted when M.L. arrived at southwest Chicago's Marquette Park to lead a march to nearby real estate firms that discriminated against blacks. The roughly one thousand police officers didn't faze the several thousand whites determined to deter the march with rocks, bottles, bricks, cherry bombs, racial slurs, and menacing signs, one of which called for the extermination of blacks. Another read, "King Would Look Good With a Knife in His Back." A knife was thrown, but it didn't hit M.L. A rock, however, struck his right temple.

M.L. vowed to march again. And again. "I have to do this—to expose myself— to bring this hate into the open," he told reporters. At a mass meeting days later, he exposed himself as being as human as anybody else. "I'm tired of marching, tired of marching for something that should have been mine at first . . . I'm tired of the tensions surrounding our days . . . I'm tired of living every day under the threat of death." He ached to live a long life, but "sometimes I begin to doubt whether I'm going to make it through. I must confess, I'm tired." Even in baring some of his soul, the context was commitment. "I don't march because I like it, I march because I must."

It seemed that no amount of marching would bring major change to Chicago. Scenes of white mobs during the Marquette Park march and other demonstrations in and around Chicago had not triggered the sort of outrage from liberal whites in the North as events in Birmingham and elsewhere in the South. Some who had supported M.L.'s Southern campaigns had lost interest in the civil rights

AUGUST 5, 1966: IN MARQUETTE PARK

After he was hit in the head, M.L. persevered in the march. "I have never in my life seen such hate," he said afterward. "Not in Mississippi or Alabama. This is a terrible thing."

movement, feeling that with the passage of the Civil Rights Act of 1964 and the Voting Rights Act of 1965, the battle had been won. Others were turning their energies and donations to the growing movement against America's involvement in the Vietnam War. Black riots in the North had also chilled many whites against the civil rights movement.

By the time M.L. decamped from the Chicago Freedom Movement, Operation Breadbasket had been launched in the Windy City. The operation's main goal was to motivate white-owned corporations that did brisk business in

Check Out Receipt

Essex Branch
410-887-0295
www.bcpl.info

Tuesday, October 5, 2021 7:56:15 PM
57794

Item: 31183192802277
Title: M.L.K. : journey of a King
Call no.: Children Bio KING
Due: 10/26/2021

Total items: 1

You just saved $27.95 by using your
library today.

FREE TO BE ALL IN

As of July 1, 2021, late fees no
longer assessed for overdue items!
Ask us for details or visit bcpl.info

Shelf Help: (410) 494-9063

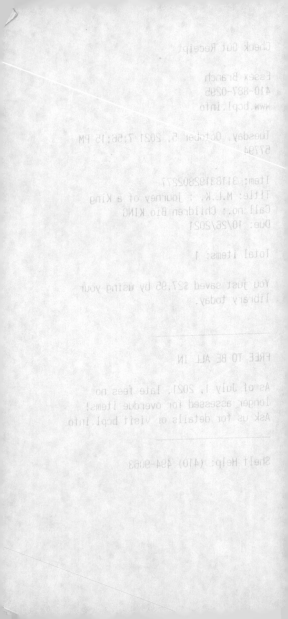

black neighborhoods to stop denying blacks job opportunities. But when it came to the city, the only thing the movement had gotten was promises. What others labeled a failure, M.L. called "a first step in a thousand mile journey."

His life was still a prayer, a testament of hope. Despite death threats from whites and the rising ridicule and rebuke from blacks—"Uncle Tom," "Martin Loser King." Still, M.L. looked at the world through the eyes of his Messiah. Still, he praised and preached *agape*, clinging to the possibility of the beloved community. He kept envisioning a day when "nobody will shout 'White Power!'—when nobody will shout 'Black Power!' —but everybody will talk about God's power and human power." That human power would be, he dreamed, healthy, healing power: power that enlightened, power that lifted people up, power infused with love, power as a tool of love. "Power at its best is love implementing the demands of justice, and justice at its best is power correcting everything that stands against love." That everything included the war in Vietnam.

America's support of South Vietnam against North Vietnam had escalated from military aid and a small corps of advisers in the early 1950s to a combat force of about four hundred thousand at a cost of billions of dollars by late 1966. This had been gnawing at M.L. for a long time, but he had yet to make a whole-soul assault against it.

Longtime friends had urged him to be more public about his antiwar stance. In June 1965, Vietnamese Buddhist monk Thich Nhat Hanh (pronounced *Tick Naught Han*) had sent him an open letter, asking the same: "I am sure that since you have been engaged in one of the hardest struggles for equality and human rights, you are among those who understand fully, and who share with

WHITE POWER!

During an August 1, 1966, Chicago Freedom Movement march, a white mob shouted of blacks, "Burn them like Jews." This photo was taken at a counter-demonstration later that month.

all their hearts, the indescribable suffering of the Vietnamese people." In talks with riot-ready youth in Chicago and elsewhere, M.L. had been brought up short by the question "What about Vietnam?" Hadn't the U.S. government resorted to violence to express its will? young blacks asked. What's more, M.L. had been literally sickened by photographs of horrors wrought by America's napalm bombs that accompanied the article "The Children of Vietnam," in the January 1967 issue of *Ramparts* magazine. Added to these promptings was his conscience calling him to recognize that if he didn't boldly denounce the war, he was no better than whites who knew in their bones that racial injustice was reprobate but said and did nothing about it.

"I oppose the war in Vietnam because I love America," M.L. said in a February 1967 address in Los Angeles. "I speak out against it not in anger but with anxiety and sorrow in my heart, and above all with a passionate desire to see our beloved country stand as the moral example of the world . . . Those of us who love peace must organize as effectively as the war hawks. As they spread the propaganda of war we must spread the propaganda of peace. We must combine the fervor of the civil rights movement with the peace movement."

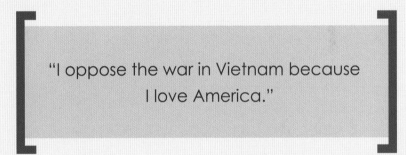

"I oppose the war in Vietnam because I love America."

M.L. delivered his best-known speech for peace at New York City's Riverside Church on April 4, 1967, at an event sponsored by Clergy and Laymen Concerned About Vietnam. In his address, he called the U.S. government out as the "greatest purveyor of violence in the world today." And he detailed the violence: millions of acres of Vietnamese rice fields devoured by flames; tens of thousands of bulldozed trees; lakes, rivers, and streams poisoned by chemicals; screams of innocents maimed and murdered by mines and napalm bombs.

M.L. rued the war's toll on American souls, too—the mounting count of American widows and orphans because of the mounting count of American soldiers coming home in body bags. Added to that, all the shattered American dreams of thousands returning "physically handicapped and psychologically deranged." M.L. knew that, relative to their percentage of the population, blacks (mostly poor blacks) were doing a disproportionate amount of the killing and dying in Vietnam—"black young men who had been crippled by our society,"

**MAY 31, 1966:
CHICAGO**

In their joint press conference, M.L. and Hanh called for America to stop bombing North Vietnam. Hanh had studied comparative religion at Princeton University, then become a teacher of the subject. His humanitarian endeavors included founding an aid organization in South Vietnam for people devastated in the war. In 1967, M.L. nominated Hanh for the Nobel Peace Prize.

sent "to guarantee liberties in Southeast Asia which they had not found in southwest Georgia and East Harlem." He bemoaned how the war robbed anti-poverty programs of resources as it devoured "men and skills and money like some demonic, destructive suction tube." He warned, "[A] nation that continues year after year to spend more money on military defense than on programs of social uplift is approaching spiritual death." He encouraged men of draft age who sincerely believed America's involvement in the war was wrong to resist the draft by seeking the status of conscientious objector.

M.L. journeyed beyond Vietnam in this speech. He upbraided the U.S. government for supporting oppressive regimes in Guatemala, South Africa, and other countries where American corporations did business, thus making profit more important than people. America "must undergo a radical revolution of values," he insisted. "We must find new ways to speak for peace in Vietnam and justice throughout the developing world . . . If we do not act, we shall surely be dragged down the long, dark, and shameful corridors of time reserved for those who possess power without compassion, might without morality, and strength without sight." In closing, he lifted up his beloved passage from the Old Testament book of Amos. "If we will but make the right choice, we will be able to speed up the day, all over America and all over the world, when justice will roll down like waters, and righteousness like a mighty stream."

Condemnation was quick—like a mighty stream. An editorial in *Life* magazine said M.L. had "gone off on a tangent." A *New York Times* editorial essentially agreed: "[T]o divert the energies of the civil rights movement to the Vietnam issue is both wasteful and self-defeating." The NAACP decried any link-up between the peace and civil rights movements, calling it a "serious tactical mistake." President Johnson was furious with M.L. and felt betrayed, as if his past support of civil rights legislation and anti-poverty programs was reason enough for M.L. to keep his mouth shut about the war.

M.L. refused to mute his message on what he had called the "madness of Vietnam" at Riverside Church. He joined forces with prominent antiwar activists in animating more Americans to get aboard the peace train. Some people insist this marks the start of M.L.'s move to left-wing politics, while others see it as more about a move into deeper dimensions of his faith.

**APRIL 15, 1967:
NEW YORK CITY**

United Nations Plaza was the destination point for an antiwar rally that began in Central Park. The rally was one of a series of demonstrations coordinated by a coalition called the Spring Mobilization to End the War in Vietnam. M.L. had already addressed the crowd. He and Stokely Carmichael hugged before the latter made his speech. Their relationship was strained but not destroyed after Carmichael's embrace of the Black Power ethic. Similarly, Julian Bond, who once dismissed M.L. as merely a "preacher who can talk well," later hailed him as "the twentieth century's greatest civic leader."

Spring 1967 was another season of motion and strain. M.L. had committed to a plethora of speaking engagements in places as different as San Francisco, Denver, and Geneva, Switzerland. He went to Chicago, Cleveland, and Louisville more than once for meetings on programs and protests SCLC cosponsored. He made the media rounds to promote his book *Where Do We Go from Here: Chaos or Community?*, another plea for the beloved community, locally and globally. "Every nation must now develop an overriding loyalty to mankind as a whole in order to preserve the best in their individual societies. This call for a world-wide fellowship that lifts neighborly concern beyond one's tribe, race, class and nation is in reality a call for an all-embracing and unconditional love for all men." Love, he contended, was "an absolute necessity" for the survival of the human race. "Love is the key which unlocks the door that leads to ultimate reality. This Hindu-Moslem-Christian-Jewish-Buddhist belief about ultimate reality is beautifully summed up in the First Epistle of Saint John: 'Let us love one another: for love is of God: and every one that loveth is born of God, and knoweth God . . .' Let us hope that this spirit will become the order of the day." It didn't.

Chaos hit. For the third summer in a row, inner cities flamed. "Only drastic changes in the life of the poor will provide the kind of order and stability you desire," read M.L.'s telegram to President Johnson on July 25, day three of riots in Detroit.

By then, M.L. was thoroughly convinced that nothing would save the soul of America except a radical restructuring of its economic system. He wanted SCLC to ratchet up from advancing a "reform movement" to advancing a "revolutionary" one. He envisioned another march on Washington, one that stressed a problem plaguing millions of Americans of all descents: poverty. In the richest nation in the world, nearly thirty million of its citizens—close to fifteen percent of the population—lived in pounding poverty: so many souls, too many souls, going without sufficient nutrition, without visits to physicians and dentists, without eyeglasses, without heat in winter, without sleep at night to keep rats from attacking their children.

"Repent, America!" became the motto of this march on Washington—the Poor People's Campaign. M.L. dreamed of a multicultural multitude of poor folk camping out in the nation's capital until demands were met. A guaranteed life-sustaining, dignity-inducing income for every American adult was at the top of the list.

Cynics thought M.L.'s entrance into the antiwar movement and his call for a Poor People's Campaign sprang from his need to be in the limelight, to reinvent

DIALOGUE

After the U.N. rally, its leaders met with the U.N.'s Ralph Bunche (seated to right of desk). Left to right: Reverend Jim Bevel, organizer of Birmingham's Children's Crusade; Dave Dellinger, longtime antiwar activist; Dr. Benjamin Spock; Cleveland Robinson, labor union leader; M.L.; Dagmar Wilson, cofounder of Women's Strike for Peace, of which Coretta was a member. On April 15, Coretta addressed the antiwar rally in San Francisco.

himself now that the Black Power movement was eclipsing the movement he symbolized. Such people might have been persuaded otherwise had they heard him preach at Ebenezer on the first Sunday in February 1968. His text was in the Gospel of Mark, the moment where two of Jesus' disciples, brothers James and John, ask for high places of honor by his side in heaven. M.L. explained that these earnest but still spiritually immature men were afflicted with the need to be number one—the "drum major instinct." Unchecked, it spawned countless wrongs, from boasting and living above your means to scorning people in need.

There was only one thing worth striving to be number one in, M.L. maintained: *agape*. He then turned to death, his death. He said he sometimes thought about his funeral and wondered, "What is it that I would want said?"

"I'd like somebody to mention that day that Martin Luther King, Jr., tried to give his life serving others. I'd like for somebody to say that day, that Martin Luther King, Jr., tried to love somebody. I want you to say that day that I tried to be right on the war question."

Drum major?

"Yes, if you want to say that I was a drum major, say that I was a drum major for justice; say that I was a drum major for peace; I was a drum major for righteousness. And all of the other shallow things will not matter. I won't have any money to leave behind. I won't have the fine and luxurious things of life to leave behind. But I just want to leave a committed life behind. And that's all I want to say."

> "I'd like somebody to mention that day that Martin Luther King, Jr., tried to give his life serving others. I'd like for somebody to say that day that Martin Luther King, Jr., tried to love somebody."

He suffered sleepless nights. He was mauled by migraines, dogged by depression. Prayer power seemed to be on empty.

Financial backers had fallen away. Some colleagues complained that he was making a serious mistake, reaching for too much change. But nothing could turn him around, keep him from traveling the country to raise support for the Poor People's Campaign, set for late April.

Though M.L.'s time was tight, he couldn't say no when Reverend Jim Lawson, SNCC cofounder, Freedom Rider, SCLC colleague, and friend, asked him to lend his presence to a movement in Memphis. That city's black sanitation workers had gone on strike, seeking a pay raise, benefits, and respect. City officials had ignored their demands, treating them like invisible men.

M.L. arrived in Memphis on March 18 to deliver the fourteenth of more than thirty speeches he would give that week. "Nothing worthwhile is gained without sacrifice," he told the roughly fifteen thousand people who packed the Church of God in Christ's Mason Temple. He admitted that he was at times dispirited and beset with the feeling that his work was in vain, "but then the Holy Spirit revives my soul again." Before he left, M.L. promised to return for a march.

Ten days later, the march was on, with about six thousand souls, some of whom were brash young men bearing "Black Power Is Here" signs. The march was only a few blocks along when violence shattered peace. M.L. was whisked away as bricks and bottles crashed plate-glass windows.

Back at his hotel, M.L. was soul sick to the point of getting physically ill, grieved to the point of tears. "Maybe we just have to admit that the day of violence is here, and maybe we have to just give up and let violence take its course," he told Abernathy. M.L.'s critics blamed him for the madness of the march. They predicted that the Poor People's Campaign would turn violent.

A few days later, back in Atlanta, M.L.'s soul was revived again. Against the advice of close colleagues, he was determined to lead another march in Memphis, insisting that nonviolence could and would prevail.

Memphis was coming out from under the blows of a thunderstorm when M.L. returned on Wednesday, April 3. Running a slight fever and wearied by the bomb threat that had delayed their flight, he asked Abernathy to speak in his stead at that night's rally at Mason Temple. Later, when he got the call in his room at the Lorraine Motel that the people desperately wanted a message from him, he got into a suit and went out into the Memphis night wet again with rain and under tornado watch.

M.L. offered the crowd more than encouragement. He called them to concrete action beyond the march set for April 8. To marching they needed to add economic pressure, such as a "bank-in" movement: for blacks to close their accounts in white-owned banks and deposit their money in black-owned ones. "You have six or seven black insurance companies here in the city of Memphis. Take out your insurance there. We want to have an 'insurance-in.'" Deeper into the speech, M.L. urged the crowd to "rise up tonight with a greater readiness. Let us stand with a greater determination. And let us move on in these powerful days, these days of challenge to make America what it ought to be." His eyes were still on the prize of the Promised Land. "I may not get there with you. But I want you to know tonight, that we, as a people will get to the Promised Land. And so I'm happy, tonight. I'm not worried about *any*thing. I'm not fearing *any* man. Mine eyes have seen the *glo-ry* of the coming of the Lord."

Another rally was scheduled for the next night. Before that, M.L. was looking forward to dinner with friends. Around six o'clock, he stepped onto the balcony outside his motel room, expecting Abernathy to join him any minute and exchanging pleasantries with colleagues in the courtyard below. One of them was musician Ben Branch, of whom he asked a favor regarding a song by Thomas Dorsey, the "father of gospel music," composed when he was dealing with a double death: that of his wife and just-born baby. It's a song confessing frailty—*I'm tired, I'm weak, I'm worn.* It's a song professing faith—*lead me on to the light.* It's a song of surrender to a power mightier than the self.

> "[R]ise up tonight with a greater readiness. Let us stand with a greater determination. And let us move on in these powerful days, these days of challenge to make America what it ought to be."

"Ben, make sure you play 'Precious Lord, Take My Hand' in the meeting tonight."

Seconds later, some of M.L.'s friends heard what they thought was a firecracker. Others thought a car had backfired.

Oh.

THURSDAY, APRIL 4, 1968

The bullet severed M.L.'s spinal cord. About a year later, a white petty thief, James Earl Ray, was sentenced to ninety-nine years in prison for killing M.L.

**APRIL 9, 1968:
ATLANTA**

Five days after M.L.'s assassination, upward of fifty thousand people crowded around Ebenezer Baptist Church. Inside, about eight hundred—family members, close friends, VIPs—witnessed M.L.'s home-going service. The program included excerpts from his tape-recorded sermon about the drum major instinct: *Say that I was a drum major for justice, say that I was a drum major for peace.* After this service, his body was transported to Morehouse for a public ceremony where Benjamin Mays delivered the eulogy and Mahalia Jackson sang "Precious Lord" before more than one hundred thousand mourners. Coretta led the roughly four-mile, sun-baked march across town to Morehouse. With her, left to right: her first-born, Yolanda Denise, age twelve; her brother-in-law, A.D.; her youngest child, Bernice Albertine, age five; Reverend Abernathy; and her sons, Dexter Scott and Martin Luther III, ages seven and ten. The children were with their mother the day before when she led the Memphis march in their father's stead.

AUTHOR'S NOTE

I was nine when M.L. was killed. I don't remember where I was when I heard the news, or the tone in my home later that night, or anything my parents said the next day, or the next, or the day of his funeral. All I've ever been able to retrieve from memory about those April 1968 days is the sight of a teacher at East Harlem's M.E.S. 146—an imposing, she-who-must-be-obeyed type—with tears on the rise at the mention of his name.

I mean no disrespect by calling him M.L. It's about recognizing that I grew up regarding "the Reverend Dr. Martin Luther King, Jr." as more statue than man: someone I revered but to whom I couldn't relate, and so I did not truly appreciate him. To some extent, this book is my soul's journey into why that teacher at my elementary school cried, and why I sometimes wept as I listened to his sermons and speeches, read his writings, and processed others' written and visual renderings of his life in my search to see, to feel the man: someone who could have lived a relatively comfortable life, but instead spent thousands of hours, thousands of days—what turned out to be the last thirteen years of his life—marching, preaching, praying for a righteous America. All the while—a bull's-eye on his back.

And he—Dr. King, Rev., Michael, Mike, Martin, M.L.—he was the first to state that he was not a saint but a "sinner," shorthand for one who misses the mark when it comes to perfection. I chose not to detail his flaws because I was hard-pressed to see how that helps us focus on "the dream," which is what I think he would want, what I think we need.

I was in the middle of this book in the summer of 2005 when Hurricane Katrina hit, billboarding America's rot. Tens of thousands of people were left to fend for themselves for far too long. Black, brown, white. So many were elderly; so many were children. Overwhelmingly, they were poor. I stopped work on this book, feeling, what's the point? Wondering, does anyone really care about "the dream"?

One of the things that helped me get back on track is another something Hurricane Katrina revealed, as did 9/11, as does the existence of shelters and food pantries and clothing banks. It is that America abounds with people who reflexively rise up for rescue in times of disaster, offering their time, talent, and treasure for the sake of people they may not know—caring, sharing, trying to bind up wounds, not giving a hoot about color, class, gender, sexuality, religion, or politics. I believe that this speaks to the seed of a sense of the beloved community, a longing to live *agapic*, an ache for the dream to be real.

May you do your part.

LIFE

WEEK OF SHOCK

▸Vietnam: Burst of Hope
▸Convulsion in U.S. Politics

▸EXCLUSIVE PICTURES
The Murder in Memphis

Martin Luther King
1929–1968

APRIL 12 · 1968 · 35¢

IN MEMORIAM

The title of the sermon he planned to preach at Ebenezer on Sunday, April 7: "Why America May Go to Hell."

TIME LINE

SELECTED MOMENTS FROM THE CONTEXT OF M.L.'S LIFE

1929

- M.L. is born in Atlanta on January 15.
- Stock market crash in October triggers the Great Depression.
- National Urban League launches a "Don't Buy Where You Can't Work" campaign in Chicago.

1930

- Fannie Peck, first lady of Detroit's Bethel African Methodist Episcopal Church, forms Housewives' League to increase support of black-owned businesses and to boycott white-owned ones that refused to hire blacks.
- In Detroit, Wallace Fard founds what becomes the Nation of Islam, which will promote black separatism and the idea that whites are devils.
- The Black Shirts, a white supremacist organization, forms in Atlanta. The group mounts a "No Jobs for Niggers Until Every White Man Has a Job!" campaign.

1931

- M.L.'s grandfather A.D. Williams dies.
- Nine young black men are jailed in Scottsboro, Alabama, after two young white women falsely accuse them of rape. The nine are tried with inept counsel and are found guilty. The railroading of the "Scottsboro Boys" outrages proponents of racial justice.
- In Omaha, Nebraska, Georgia-born Baptist minister Earl Little, an organizer for Marcus Garvey's Universal Negro Improvement Association, dies in a freak accident. His son Malcolm (later Malcolm X) will assert that he was murdered by white supremacists.

1932

- M.L. enters nursery school.
- Myles Horton founds Highlander Folk School in Monteagle, Tennessee. This adult-education center trains union and civil rights activists. Rosa Parks will attend a workshop in 1955.

1933

- The NAACP files a suit on behalf of Thomas Hocutt, whom the University of North Carolina's pharmacy school denied admission because he was black.
- M.L. begins first grade at Yonge Street Elementary School, along with his sister, age six. He is expelled in January 1934 after he spills the beans to his teacher that he is only five.

1934

· Georgia-born Elijah Muhammad becomes the leader of the Nation of Islam, headquartered in Chicago.
· The National Football League begins a ban on black players that lasts until the mid-1940s.

1935

· In late January, M.L. enters first grade again; he will start second grade in September 1935.
· Martin Luther King, Sr., leads a protest at the Fulton County Courthouse against the segregation of elevators. He later heads up a voter registration drive in Atlanta.
· Charles Hamilton Houston, a graduate of Harvard Law School and vice-dean of Howard University's law school, becomes the NAACP's special counsel. He takes the legal campaign for racial justice to a new level. Former student Thurgood Marshall becomes his deputy.
· The Maryland Court of Appeals orders the University of Maryland to admit Donald Murray, a black graduate of Amherst. The lawsuit was handled by the NAACP.

1936

· The NAACP files *Gibbs v. Board of Education* in Montgomery County, Maryland, for equal pay for black and white teachers.
· M.L. begins third grade at David T. Howard Elementary School.

1937

· M.L. becomes an *Atlanta Journal* paperboy.

· The KKK parades on Auburn Avenue, in Atlanta.

1938

· Martin Luther King, Sr., joins the Atlanta Civic and Political League's executive committee.
· Thurgood Marshall becomes the NAACP's special counsel.
· In *Missouri ex rel. Gaines v. Canada*, the U.S. Supreme Court rules that Missouri cannot pay for a black person to attend a law school out of state to avoid admitting that person to an in-state law school. The plaintiff's case was handled by the NAACP.

1939

· More than 75,000 attend Marian Anderson's early-April concert at the Lincoln Memorial, arranged with the help of First Lady Eleanor Roosevelt after the Daughters of the American Revolution refused to allow Anderson to have a concert in D.C.'s Constitution Hall.

1940

· Thurgood Marshall forms a separate legal arm of the NAACP: the NAACP Legal Defense and Educational Fund, Inc. (LDF).
· Pauli Murray, a member of Fellowship of Reconciliation, is arrested and jailed for refusing to sit in the back of an interstate bus in Virginia. Murray will become the first black to earn a doctorate from Yale Law School and the Episcopal Church's first black woman priest.

1941

- M.L. enters Atlanta University's Laboratory School.
- In *Hansberry v. Lee*, the U.S. Supreme Court upholds Carl Hansberry's right to a home he purchased in an exclusive Chicago suburb that had a ban on black residents. The Hansberry family's drama and trauma before and after the ruling is the basis for daughter Lorraine's award-winning play *A Raisin in the Sun* (1959).

- Labor union leader A. Philip Randolph starts organizing a massive march on Washington, D.C., to protest racial discrimination in plants and factories with defense contracts. He calls off the march after President Franklin D. Roosevelt issues Executive Order 8802 in late June. It creates the Fair Employment Practices Committee.
- The U.S. Army launches a pilot-training program for blacks at Tuskegee, Alabama, genesis of the Tuskegee Airmen.
- Race riots erupt in East St. Louis, Illinois.
- M.L.'s maternal grandmother dies.
- The KKK holds a convention in Atlanta.
- The Japanese attack on Pearl Harbor triggers the U.S. entry into World War II.

1942

- An interracial group of students at the University of Chicago founds what becomes the Congress of Racial Equality (CORE).
- M.L. enters tenth grade at Booker T. Washington High.

1943

- CORE stages its first sit-in, at Jack Spratt's Coffee Shop in Chicago.
- Detroit suffers the worst race riots of the 1940s.

1944

- In *Smith v. Allwright*, the U.S. Supreme Court outlaws all-white primaries maintained by the Democratic Party in Texas. Thurgood Marshall is the plaintiff's lead lawyer.
- M.L. delivers the speech "The Negro and the Constitution" in Dublin, Georgia, and enters Morehouse a few months later.

1945

- The U.S. drops atomic bombs on Hiroshima and Nagasaki, Japan, in early August. World War II soon ends.

1946

- In *Morgan v. Virginia*, the U.S. Supreme Court outlaws segregated seating on interstate buses.
- M.L. quits his job with the Railway Express Company because a supervisor called him "nigger."
- Prompted in part by the racially motivated murders of several black World War II veterans, President Harry S. Truman creates the President's Committee on Civil Rights.

1947

- M.L. becomes chair of the local NAACP Youth Council membership committee.
- Fellowship of Reconciliation organizes black and white teams to ride buses into

the South to test the *Morgan v. Virginia* decision. During their "Journey of Reconciliation," pioneer Freedom Riders suffer physical attacks and arrests.
· Jackie Robinson is the first black to play on a Major League baseball team (Brooklyn Dodgers) since the late nineteenth century.
· A. Philip Randolph cofounds the Committee Against Jim Crow in Military Service and Training.

1948

· The NAACP LDF triumphs in *Sipuel v. Board of Regents of Oklahoma*. The U.S. Supreme Court rules that states cannot deny blacks admission to their publicly funded law schools if they do not have a law school for blacks. In the years that follow, the LDF will handle dozens more lawsuits against segregation, most involving public schools and institutions of higher learning.
· President Truman issues Executive Order 9981, mandating "equality of treatment and opportunity for all persons in the armed services without regard to race, color, religion or national origin." Integration within the U.S. armed forces becomes a reality in the 1950s.
· While in prison, Malcolm Little (Malcolm X) becomes intrigued with the Nation of Islam, becoming a member in 1953.
· M.L. begins his first year at Crozer Theological Seminary.

1950

· The U.S. enters the conflict between North and South Korea in June after the Soviet-Union-backed Communist regime in North Korea invades South Korea.

1951

· CORE launches sit-ins in Baltimore.
· Barbara Johns rallies fellow students at her high school in Farmville, Virginia, to boycott the school in protest of its unequal conditions relative to the high school for whites. The three-day strike leads to a lawsuit for integration. The case is one of five cases bundled into *Brown v. Board of Education*. Barbara Johns's uncle, Vernon Johns, is the activist-preacher who preceded M.L. as pastor of Dexter Avenue Baptist Church.
· M.L. graduates from Crozer with a bachelor of divinity degree.
· Civil rights activists Harry and Henrietta Moore are killed when their home in Mims, Florida, is bombed.
· A race riot erupts in Cicero, Illinois, after whites attack the home of a black family that moved into a "white" neighborhood.

1952

· M.L. and Coretta Scott begin to date.
· The U.S. Supreme Court starts hearing arguments in *Brown v. Board of Education*.

1953

· The U.S. Supreme Court outlaws segregation in D.C. restaurants.
· M.L. and Coretta Scott marry.
· The Korean War ends.
· Whites terrorize a black family that moved into Trumbull Park Homes, a

public housing complex in Chicago. Riots ensue after other black families move into Trumbull.

1954

• In Indianola, Mississippi, a group of white men (among them entrepreneurs, lawyers, and ministers) form the White Citizens Council (WCC) to marshal resistance to the *Brown* decision and repress black aspirations for civil rights. WCCs soon form in other states. Other groups formed in reaction to *Brown* include the American States Rights Association and the National Association for the Advancement of White People.

• Milford, Delaware's public school system closes after whites protest the attempt of eleven black students to enroll in Milford High School. When the school system reopens a few days later, about 70 percent of white students boycott school. Attempts to desegregate the school are tabled.

• M.L. is installed as pastor of Dexter Avenue Baptist Church.

1955

• Nearly 150,000 congregations participate in the National Council of Churches (NCC) Race Relations Sunday.

• Claudette Colvin, a student at Montgomery's Booker T. Washington High School and an NAACP Youth Council member, is arrested after refusing to give up her bus seat to a white man several months before Rosa Parks makes her stand.

• In the ruling known as *Brown II*, the

U.S. Supreme Court orders public schools to be integrated "with all deliberate speed." The ambiguity of the language allows school officials who are die-hard segregationists to drag their feet on desegregation.

• M.L. receives his Ph.D. in systematic theology from Boston University.

• Georgia's board of education makes a teacher's membership in the NAACP grounds for dismissal.

• Fourteen-year-old Emmett Till is brutally murdered in Money, Mississippi, for allegedly getting fresh with a white woman. Till's murder and the easy acquittal of the men charged with killing him propel countless people to join the civil rights crusade.

• Eighteen-year-old Mary Louise Smith is arrested for refusing to give up her seat on a Montgomery city bus for a white person two months before Rosa Parks makes her stand.

1956

• Autherine Lucy is suspended from the University of Alabama after whites riot over her enrollment.

• More than one hundred members of the U.S. Congress sign the "Southern Manifesto," denouncing the *Brown* decision.

• A black bus boycott in Tallahassee, Florida, begins in late May and ends two years later when segregated seating on buses ends.

• Septima Clark is fired from her teaching job in Charleston, South Carolina, because she refused to end her NAACP membership. She becomes

director of workshops at Highlander Folk School in Tennessee. SCLC will absorb Clark's program after the U.S. government shuts down Highlander.
• The NAACP is banned from operating in Alabama.
• M.L. celebrates the abolition of segregated buses in Alabama.

1957

• M.L. gives his first national address, at the Prayer Pilgrimage.
• Arkansas governor Orval Faubus is in the forefront of opposition to the integration of Central High School in Little Rock, Arkansas. The "Little Rock Nine" begin attending Central after President Dwight D. Eisenhower provides federal troop protection.
• In Nashville, Hattie Cotton Elementary School is bombed in protest of integration.

1958

• M.L.'s first book, *Stride Toward Freedom*, is published.
• NAACP Youth Council members launch lunch-counter sit-ins in Wichita, Kansas, and Oklahoma City, Oklahoma.
• About ten thousand young people turn out for Youth March for Integrated Schools in Washington, D.C. Coretta delivers a message from M.L.

1959

• M.L. journeys to India.
• Virginia's Prince Edward County closes public schools rather than integrate them.

1960

• Atlanta becomes M.L.'s home again.
• A race riot erupts when several dozen blacks stage a "wade-in" at a beach in Biloxi, Mississippi.
• President Eisenhower signs the Civil Rights Act of 1960. Among other things, it establishes penalties (fines or imprisonment) for violating a person's voting rights.
• In *Boynton v. Virginia*, the U.S. Supreme Court outlaws segregation in interstate transportation facilities.

1961

• Charlayne Hunter and Hamilton Holmes endure mob menace and a temporary suspension of their lawsuit-won right to attend the University of Georgia at Athens. She will become an award-winning print and broadcast journalist; he, a physician.
• President John F. Kennedy issues Executive Order 10925, creating a committee to investigate racial discrimination by companies with government contracts.
• Bob Moses and fellow SNCC members launch the Voter Education Project in McComb, Mississippi. Farmer Herbert Lee, who works with them, is one of the first casualties of the endeavor: A state legislator shoots him dead, claiming self-defense. An eyewitness is killed before he can testify.

1962

• In his State of the Union address, President Kennedy urges Congress to create legislation outlawing literacy

tests and poll taxes as qualifications for voting.
• In Brownsville, Tennessee, a tent city goes up for black sharecroppers evicted from their homes for trying to register to vote.
• M.L. becomes involved with the Albany Movement.
• Mississippi governor Ross Barnett stymies James Meredith's right to attend "Ole Miss" (the University of Mississippi in Oxford). Whites riot after Meredith registers at Ole Miss under the protection of federal marshals. President Kennedy calls for troops on the scene to maintain order.
• The Cuban Missile Crisis: For fourteen days in October, people fear nuclear war will result from the standoff between the USSR and the U.S. over the former's installation of nuclear missiles in Cuba.
• President Kennedy signs Executive Order 11063, banning discrimination in housing owned and funded by the federal government and constructed with the help of loans from a federal government agency.

1963

• In February, A. Philip Randolph announces plans for a March on Washington.
• M.L. becomes involved in the Birmingham campaign.
• Medgar Evers, the NAACP's field secretary in Mississippi, launches sit-ins and demonstrations in Jackson in late May. Evers is assassinated in June, the day after President Kennedy's

televised address on civil rights.
• Governor George Wallace stands in the doorway of the administration building of the University of Alabama in Tuscaloosa to prevent two blacks, Vivian Malone and James Hood, from registering. After the U.S. attorney general orders the school to let the students enroll, they do.
• M.L. delivers "I Have a Dream" at the March on Washington.
• Roughly 200,000 young black Chicagoans protest the inferiority of their schools by boycotting them.

1964

• The 24th Amendment becomes a part of the U.S. Constitution. It outlaws denying a person the right to vote because of failure to pay any kind of tax.
• Blacks riot in Cambridge, Maryland, in reaction to police brutality and other humiliations.
• Malcolm X leaves the Nation of Islam.
• Fannie Lou Hamer cofounds the Mississippi Freedom Democratic Party (MFDP). At the National Democratic Convention in Atlantic City, MFDP challenges the legitimacy of the delegates from the state's whites–only Democratic Party.
• In Vicksburg, Mississippi, two black churches, which served as voter registration centers, are bombed.
• M.L. receives the Nobel Peace Prize.

1965

• M.L. begins his involvement with the voting rights campaign in Selma.

- The first U.S. combat troops are sent to Vietnam.
- Malcolm X is assassinated.
- Between late March and June 1, antiwar activists hold a major teach-in at the University of Michigan; about 25,000 turn out for an antiwar rally in D.C.; an antiwar teach-in is broadcast at more than one hundred campuses; and about 30,000 attend a thirty-six-hour teach-in on Vietnam at the University of California at Berkeley.
- President Lyndon Baines Johnson issues Executive Order 11246, compelling companies with government contracts to "take affirmative action" to see to it that job applicants and employees are not discriminated against because of "race, creed, color, or national origin."
- About 20,000 attend the March on Washington for Peace in Vietnam.

1966

- M.L. becomes very involved in the Chicago Freedom Movement.
- Julian Bond, duly elected to Georgia's House of Representatives, is denied his seat because of his outspoken opposition to the Vietnam War. He is eventually seated as the result of a lawsuit.
- Huey Newton and Bobby Seale found the Black Panther Party in Oakland, California.

1967

- M.L. delivers the "Beyond Vietnam" speech at New York City's Riverside Church.

- Muhammad Ali is stripped of his heavyweight boxing title for refusing the draft.
- An antiwar demonstration in D.C. draws a crowd of about 50,000.

1968

- President Johnson announces on March 31 that he will not run for reelection. Vietnam, now widely recognized as unwinnable, has driven the president to depression and despair.
- M.L. is murdered. Blacks in more than one hundred cities riot in reaction.
- Four days after M.L.'s murder, Michigan Representative John Conyers, Jr., presents legislation for a federal holiday in M.L.'s honor.
- Seven days after M.L.'s murder, President Johnson signs the Fair Housing Act.
- In mid-May, the Poor People's Campaign commences with Ralph Abernathy at the helm of SCLC. Protesters live in "Resurrection City," a crowd of tents and shacks on the National Mall in Washington, D.C. Inhabitants include blacks, whites, Hispanics, and Native Americans. When the Poor People's Campaign ends in mid-June, it is deemed a failure.
- Coretta Scott King founds the Martin Luther King, Jr., Center for Nonviolent Social Change.

In 1983, Congress passes, and President Ronald Reagan signs, a bill making the third Monday of every January the Martin Luther King, Jr., National Holiday, starting in 1986.

NOTES

Part I

On "Oh." Photographer Joseph Louw, quoted in "Martin Luther King," *Life* magazine, April 12, 1968, p. 76.

"You are . . . my foot." Unidentified woman, quoted in *The Autobiography of Martin Luther King, Jr.*, p. 9.

"How . . . me?" King, quoted in *The Autobiography*, p. 7.

"[T]he shouting . . . me." King, quoted in *Time* magazine, January 3, 1964. Accessed at TIME Archive: www.time.com/time/magazine/archives.

"many . . . escape." King, "An Autobiography of Religious Development," in *The Papers of Martin Luther King, Jr.*, vol. 1, p. 362.

"Both . . . to be." King, quoted in *The Papers*, vol. 1, p. 44.

King's sermon at Dexter. "Address to Dexter Avenue Baptist Church Congregation, Montgomery, May 2, 1954," reprinted in *The Autobiography*, pp. 45–46. King's installation was held in fall 1954.

"Let . . . awhile." King, quoted in *Bearing the Cross*, p. 17.

"with . . . anxiety" and "a miracle . . . place." King, *Stride Toward Freedom*, pp. 52, 54.

Flyer. Women's Political Council, in *The Montgomery Bus Boycott and the Women Who Started It*, pp. 45–46.

"I turned . . . ever." King, *Stride*, p. 59.

"something . . . born." Parks, Introduction to "Address to the First Montgomery Improvement Association (MIA) Mass Meeting," in *A Call to Conscience*, p. 2.

Order of events at mass meeting. *The Papers*, vol. 3, p. 71.

King's December 5, 1955, address. "Address to the First Montgomery Improvement Association (MIA) Mass Meeting," in *A Call to Conscience*, pp. 7–12.

"If one day . . . so far." King, *Stride Toward Freedom*, p. 133.

Threatening phone call. Unidentified man, quoted in *Bearing the Cross*, p. 57.

On King's crisis in his kitchen. King, *Stride Toward Freedom*, pp. 134–35.

On the lawsuit. Aurelia Browder, Susie McDonald, Claudette Colvin, and Mary Louise Smith, all of whom had suffered injustice on a city bus, were the plaintiffs in the case *Browder v. Gayle*. The defendants included Montgomery's mayor, W.A. Gayle, its chief of police, and Montgomery City Lines. In early June 1956, a panel of three judges in a U.S District Court ruled in favor of the plaintiffs. Defendants appealed.

"Now let's . . . love" and "on . . . corroding hate." King, *Stride Toward Freedom*, pp. 138, 139.

"I must . . . return." King, *Stride Toward Freedom*, p. 145.

"You're . . . son." Mays, quoted in *To the Mountaintop*, p. 75.

Correspondence from Franklin, et al. *The Papers*, vol. 3, pp. 116, 117, 119, 130–31, 134, 137–38, 146, 148, 168–70.

On King's March 22, 1956, conviction. In late January 1957, weeks after the boycott ended, M.L.'s appeal was denied because his attorney missed a filing deadline. M.L. decided to pay the fine. Around the same time, Montgomery prosecutors dismissed the cases against the other MIA leaders. Their trials had been put on hold pending the outcome of M.L.'s case.

"The protest . . . approach." *The Papers*, vol. 3, pp. 200–01.

"Christ furnished . . . method." King, "An Experiment in Love," in *A Testament of Hope*, p. 17.

"[T]he end is . . . community." King, "Facing the Challenge of a New Age," in *The Papers*, vol. 3, p. 458.

"I would . . . a nigger." Unidentified man, quoted in *The Autobiography*, p. 98.

On the mid-January 1957 mass meeting. *Stride Toward Freedom*, p. 178.

"Bob . . . tonight." King, quoted in *Parting the Waters*, p. 201.

Part II

"Across the South . . . of men." "Attack on the Conscience," *Time* magazine, February 18, 1957. Accessed at TIME Archive: www.time.com/time/magazine/archives.

"Help me . . . born." King, quoted in *The Papers*, vol. 4, p. v.

"I think . . . world." King, quoted in an interview by Etta Moten Barnett, in *The Papers*, vol. 4, p. 146.

Excerpt from "Give Us the Ballot." *A Call to Conscience*, p. 48.

On Izola Ware Curry. She accused M.L. of sabotaging her faith (Roman Catholic), among other things. Curry was committed to a hospital for the criminally insane in Beacon, New York.

"Don't prosecute . . . healed." King, quoted in *Let the Trumpet Sound*, p. 140.

"Everything . . . all right." King, quoted in *Parting the Waters*, p. 244.

Easter Sunday 1959 sermon. "A Walk Through the Holy Land," in *The Papers*, vol. 5, pp. 164–75.

"to meditate . . . struggle ahead." King, April 18, 1960, letter in *The Papers*, vol. 5, p. 436.

"intellectually" and "emotional involvement." King, quoted in *The Papers*, vol. 5, p. 31.

"to retreat . . . determination." King, "Suffering and Faith," in *The Papers*, vol. 5, p. 444.

"Our . . . beloved community." King, "Statement at Founding Conference of the Student Nonviolent Coordinating Committee," in *The Autobiography*, p. 140.

"I . . . preached." King, quoted in *Parting the Waters*, p. 352.

"bring . . . the Negro." King, "Why We Chose Jail, Not Bail: Statement to judge after the arrests at Rich's, Atlanta, October 19, 1960," in *The Autobiography*, p. 145.

"M.L. . . . right." Martin Luther King, Sr., quoted in *Parting the Waters*, p. 357.

"Corrie . . . strong," King, quoted in *My Life with Martin Luther King, Jr.*, p. 178.

"King, get up!" Jailer, quoted in *Parting the Waters*, p. 360.

King's letter to his wife. *The Papers*, vol. 5, pp. 531–32.

"I think . . . Golgotha." King, quoted in *Parting the Waters*, p. 467.

"God Bless you," "Do you . . . demonstrate?" and "We . . . City Hall." Anderson, Pritchett, and King, quoted in *Parting the Waters*, p. 548.

"If . . . join me." King, quoted in *Parting the Waters*, p. 551.

"a devastating . . . face." *New York Herald Tribune*, quoted in *Parting the Waters*, p. 557.

"I paid . . . I want." Quarterman, quoted in "Kennedy: The Reluctant Emancipator," by Howard Zinn. *The Nation*, December 1, 1962, p. 374.

"turn Albany upside down." King, quoted in *Eyes on the Prize*, p. 173.

"The world . . . tonight" and "I've heard . . . ninety-nine years." Wells, quoted in *Parting the Waters*, p. 612.

"They . . . the people." King, quoted in *Parting the Waters*, p. 613.

Telegram to Mayor Kelley. *Parting the Waters*, pp. 616–17.

"Did . . . rocks?" and "all . . . nonviolent way." Pritchett and King, quoted in *Parting the Waters*, p. 618.

"We . . . power of souls." King, quoted in *Parting the Waters*, p. 619.

"He has . . . talk well." Bond, quoted in *Black Leaders*, p. 34.

Part III

"I'm . . . man." King, quoted in *Let the Trumpet Sound*, p. 206.

"run . . . streets." Conner, quoted in *Let the Trumpet Sound*, p. 212.

"Segregation . . . forever!" Wallace, quoted in *Eyes on the Prize*, p. 183.

"I . . . march." King, quoted in *Martin Luther King, Jr.*, p. 105.

"I don't . . . light." King, *Why We Can't Wait*, p. 63.

Clerics' letter. Posted at www.stanford.edu/group/King/frequentdocs/clergy.pdf.

"Letter from Birmingham Jail." *Why We Can't Wait*, pp. 64–84.

"It makes me sick." John Kennedy, quoted in *Martin Luther King, Jr.*, p. 113.

Ten commandments. *Why We Can't Wait*, p. 51.

Kennedy's June 11, 1963, address. *The Eyes on the Prize Civil Rights Reader*, pp. 160–62.

"They came . . . love." King, *Why We Can't Wait*, p. 113.

"Tell . . . the dream!" Jackson, quoted in "Martin Luther

King Jr., 'I Have a Dream' (1963)" in USIA's Basic Readings in U.S. Democracy: http://usinfo.state.gov/usa/infousa/facts/democrac/38.htm. As books have already been published including the speech, and the cost to reproduce even only a few lines is prohibitive and beyond my book permission budget, I have chosen not to include all or a fragment herewith.

"God . . . out of evil." King, "Eulogy for the Young Victims of the Sixteenth Street Baptist Church Bombing," in *A Call to Conscience*, p. 96.

"This is . . . sick society." King, quoted in *My Life with Martin Luther King, Jr.*, p. 227.

Nobel Prize acceptance speech. "Nobel Prize Acceptance Speech," in *A Testament of Hope*, pp. 224–26.

"demands . . . injustice." Johnson, May 22, 1964, speech at the University of Michigan, Ann Arbor. Posted at Lyndon Baines Johnson Library and Museum online: http://www.lbjlib.utexas.edu/johnson/archives.hom/speeches.hom/640522.asp.

"Get . . . him!" Unidentified woman, quoted in *Let the Trumpet Sound*, p. 335.

"Go back . . . from!" Unidentified person, quoted in *Better Day Coming*, p. 297.

"I believe . . . this moment" and "You're . . . right now." King and Price, quoted in *Bearing the Cross*, p. 483.

Carmichael's "Black Power" speech. Excerpt from *The River of No Return* in *The Eyes on the Prize Civil Rights Reader*, pp. 281–82.

Quotes from and information on August 5, 1966, Marquette Park march. Branch, *At Canann's Edge*, pp. 510–11.

"I have . . . open," "I'm tired . . . must," and "a first . . . journey." King, quoted in *Bearing the Cross*, pp. 500, 515, 524.

"nobody will . . . power" and "Power . . . against love." King, "Where Do We Go From Here?," in *A Testament of Hope*, pp. 251, 247.

"I . . . Vietnamese people." Thich Nhat Hanh, quoted in *From the Beloved Community to the World House*, p. 6.

"Burn them like Jews." Mob members, quoted in *At Canann's Edge*, p. 508.

King's February 25, 1967, speech. "The Casualties of the War in Vietnam," posted at http://www.stanford.edu/group/King/publications/speeches/unpub/670225-001_The_Casualties_of_the_War_in_Vietnam.htm.

King's Riverside Church speech. "Beyond Vietnam," in *A Call to Conscience*, pp. 139–64. This speech is titled "A Time to Break Silence" in some sources.

Life editorial. "Dr. King's Disservice to His Cause," *Life* magazine, April 21, 1967, p. 4.

New York Times editorial. "Dr. King's Error," April 7, 1967, p. 36.

"serious tactical mistake." "NAACP Decries Stand of Dr. King on Vietnam," *New York Times*, April 11, 1967, p. 1.

"the . . . civic leader." Julian Bond, Foreword, *King*, p. 5.

"every nation . . . day." *Where Do We Go from Here*, pp. 190–91.

"Only drastic . . . desire," King, quoted in *Bearing the Cross*, p. 570.

"reform movement" and "revolutionary." King, quoted in *Bearing the Cross*, p. 561.

"Repent, America!" *Martin Luther King, Jr.*, p. 194.

King's February 1968 sermon. "The Drum Major Instinct," in *A Testament of Hope*, pp. 259–67.

King's March 18, 1968, speech. "Address in Memphis, Tennessee, March 18, 1968," in *The Autobiography*, pp. 353–55.

"Maybe . . . its course." King, quoted in *Bearing the Cross*, p. 611.

King's April 3, 1968, speech. "I've Been to the Mountaintop," in *A Call to Conscience*, Audio Book Tape 6. This speech is called "I've Seen the Promised Land" in some sources.

"Ben . . . tonight." King, quoted in *At Canaan's Edge*, p. 766.

Author's Note

"Why . . . Hell." *Bearing the Cross*, p. 622.

SELECTED SOURCES

Adelman, Bob, and Charles Johnson. *King: The Photobiography of Martin Luther King, Jr.*
New York: Harry N. Abrams, 2004.

Boyd, Herb. *We Shall Overcome*. Naperville, IL: Source Books Media Fusion, 2004.

Branch, Taylor. *At Canaan's Edge: America in the King Years, 1965–68*. New York:
Simon & Schuster, 2005.

——. *Parting the Waters: America in the King Years, 1954–63*. New York: Simon &
Schuster, 1988.

——. *Pillar of Fire: America in the King Years, 1963–65*. New York: Simon & Schuster, 1998.

Burns, Stewart. *To the Mountaintop: Martin Luther King, Jr.'s Sacred Mission to Save
America, 1955–1968*. New York: HarperCollins, 2004.

Carson, Clayborne, senior ed. *The Papers of Martin Luther King, Jr.*, vols. 1–5. Berkeley:
University of California Press, 1992, 1994, 1997, 2000, 2005.

——, ed. *The Autobiography of Martin Luther King, Jr.* New York: Warner, 1998.

Carson, Clayborne, David J. Garrow, Gerald Gill, Vincent Harding, Darlene Clarke Hine,
general eds. *The Eyes on the Prize Civil Rights Reader: Documents, Speeches, and
Firsthand Accounts from the Black Freedom Struggle*. New York: Penguin, 1991.

Carson, Clayborn, and Peter Holloran, eds. *A Knock at Midnight: Inspiration from the
Great Sermons of Reverend Martin Luther King, Jr.* New York: Time Warner Audio
Books, 1998.

Carson, Clayborne, and Kris Shepard, eds. *A Call to Conscience: The Landmark Speeches
of Dr. Martin Luther King, Jr.* New York: Time Warner Audio Books, 2001.

——. *A Call to Conscience: The Landmark Speeches of Dr. Martin Luther King, Jr.* New
York: Warner Books, 2001.

Collier-Thomas, Bettye, and V.P. Franklin. *My Soul Is a Witness: A Chronology of the
Civil Rights Era, 1954–1965*. New York: Henry Holt, 2000.

Fairclough, Adam. *Better Day Coming: Blacks and Equality, 1890–2000*. New York:
Penguin, 2002.

——. *To Redeem the Soul of America: The Southern Christian Leadership Conference
and Martin Luther King, Jr.* Athens, GA: University of Georgia Press, 1987.

Frady, Marshall. *Martin Luther King, Jr.* New York: Viking, 2002.

Garrow, David J. *Bearing the Cross: Martin Luther King, Jr., and the Southern Christian Leadership Conference.* New York: William Morrow, 1986.

Interfaith Youth Core. *From the Beloved Community to the World House: The Interfaith Journey of Rev. Dr. Martin Luther King, Junior.* Chicago: Interfaith Youth Core, no date. Accessed at http://www.campusquest.org/workshop/pdf/MartinLutherKingModel.pdf.

Johnson, Charles. *Dreamer: A Novel.* New York: Scribner, 1998.

Kasher, Steven. *The Civil Rights Movement: A Photographic History, 1954-1968.* New York: Abbeville Press, 1996.

King, Coretta Scott. *My Life with Martin Luther King, Jr.* revised edition. New York: Henry Holt, 1993.

King, Martin Luther, Jr. *Stride Toward Freedom: The Montgomery Story.* New York: Harper & Row, 1958.

——. *Why We Can't Wait.* New York: Signet, 2000.

——. *The Measure of a Man.* Minneapolis: Fortress Press, 2001.

——. *Where Do We Go from Here: Chaos or Community?* Boston: Beacon Press, 1968.

Martin Luther King, Jr. Research and Education Institute: http://www.stanford.edu/group/King//index.htm.

Moore, Charles, with text by Michael S. Durham. *Powerful Days: The Civil Rights Photography of Charles Moore.* New York: Stewart, Tabori & Chang, 1991.

Oates, Stephen B. *Let the Trumpet Sound: A Life of Martin Luther King, Jr.* New York: Harper Perennial, 1994.

Robinson, Jo Ann Gibson. *The Montgomery Bus Boycott and the Women Who Started It.* Knoxville: University of Tennessee Press, 1987.

Roja Productions. *Citizen King.* DVD. 2005.

Rose, Thomas, and John Greenya. *Black Leaders: Then and Now.* Garrett Park, MD: Garrett Park Press, 1984.

Schulke, Flip, and Penelope McPhee. *King Remembered: The Story of Dr. Martin Luther King, Jr. in Words and Pictures.* NewYork: Pocket Books, 1986.

Washington, James Melvin, ed. *A Testament of Hope: The Essential Writings of Martin Luther King, Jr.* New York: Harper & Row, 1986.

Williams, Juan, with the Eyes on the Prize Production Team. *Eyes on the Prize: America's Civil Rights Years, 1954-1965.* New York: Viking, 1987.

PHOTOGRAPHY CREDITS

The editors and publisher have made best efforts to obtain proper copyright clearance and credit for each of the images in the book. If an unavoidable and inadvertent error in giving proper credit occurs, it will be corrected in future editions. Photographers hold copyrights to their works.

ACKNOWLEDGMENTS

Ever grateful to the good people at Harry N. Abrams, who have contribut-ed so much to this book's being: my precious editor, Howard Reeves; his most able second, Maggie Lehrman; designer superb, Celina Carvalho; managing editor par excellence Andrea Colvin; razor-sharp assistant managing editor Scott Auerbach; sterling production manager Alexis Mentor; inimitable publicity and marketing manager Jason Wells; and gracious president and CEO Michael Jacobs. For reading and feedback on different drafts of the manuscript, thank you: Nelta Brunson Gallemore, Monalisa DeGross, Susan Hess, Kim Pearson, Ronda Penrice, Daryl Michael Scott, and Judy Dothard Simmons. Dave Jones, with the U.S. Department of Transportation Library, thanks for the documentation on that ICC ruling. Bob Adelman, thanks for the vision and the work you've done over the years; especially thanks for helping to secure the visuals in this book. Finally, thank you—thank you, Lord.

INDEX

Page numbers in *italics* indicate photographs and their captions.